Mental Models

Change Your Mind-Improving Decision-Making Skills and Critical Thinking, Solve Problems Faster and Control Your Life with Powerful Strategies, Strategic Tools and Great Mental Models

Adam Feel

© **Copyright 2019 - All rights reserved.**

The content contained within this book may not be reproduced, duplicated or transmitted without direct written permission from the author or the publisher.

Under no circumstances will any blame or legal responsibility be held against the publisher, or author, for any damages, reparation, or monetary loss due to the information contained within this book, either directly or indirectly.

Legal Notice:
This book is copyright protected. It is only for personal use. You cannot amend, distribute, sell, use, quote or paraphrase any part, or the content within this book, without the consent of the author or publisher.

Disclaimer Notice:
Please note the information contained within this document is for educational and entertainment purposes only. All effort has been executed to present accurate, up to date, reliable, complete information. No warranties of any kind are declared or implied. Readers acknowledge that the author is not engaging in the rendering of legal, financial, medical or professional advice. The content within this book has been derived from various sources. Please consult a licensed professional before attempting any techniques outlined in this book.

By reading this document, the reader agrees that under no circumstances is the author responsible for any losses, direct or indirect, that are incurred as a result of the use of information contained within this document, including, but not limited to, errors, omissions, or inaccuracies.

Table of Contents

Introduction 1
Chapter 1: The Power of Mental Models 6
    Defining Mental Models 7
    Focusing on the Process, Not the Outcome 10
    Understanding the World 14
    A Multidisciplinary Approach 18
Chapter 2: Types of Mental Models 21
    Comparative Advantage 22
    The Pareto Principle 25
    Confirmation Bias 28
    Maslow's Hierarchy of Needs 30
    Parkinson's Law 34
    10/10/10 Rule 35
    Regret Minimization Framework 37
    Eisenhower Matrix 40
    Circle of Competence 42
    Second-Order Thinking 43
    Probabilistic Thinking 45
    Inversion 46
    The Map is Not the Territory 48
Chapter 3: The Role of Mental Models 51
    Confidence in Your Approach 54
    Clarity in Direction 58
    Continuity of Strategy 60
Chapter 4: Mental Models for Clear Thinking 62
    How to Think Clearly 64
    Ideal Mental Models for Clear Thinking 69
Chapter 5: Mental Models for Critical Thinking 79
    Components of Critical Thinking 82
    Understanding Claims, Issues And Arguments 84
    Other Critical Thinking Mental Models 88
    Applying Mental Models in Critical Thinking 94
    Critical Thinking Skills Gained from Using Mental Models 100
    Analytical Skills 100
    Communication Skills 101

Creativity 101
Open-Mindedness.. 102
Problem Solving Skills 102
Chapter 6: Mental Models for Success 104
How Successful People Think 105
Confirmation Bias and Success........................... 109
Improving Productivity with Parkinson's Law 115
Improve Decision-Making with Eisenhower Matrix........ 119
Make Smart Decisions with the Circle of Competence 124
Chapter 7: Mental Models for Personal Life and Relationships 126
Key Areas Affected by Your Thoughts............................... 127
Change Your Thinking, Change Your Life 132
Work Hard to Achieve Your Goals..................................... 136
Supercharge Your Thinking with Mental Models 139
Chapter 8: Strengths and Weaknesses of Mental Models 144
Strengths of Mental Models 145
Weaknesses of Mental Models........................... 149
Chapter 9: The Relationship Between Mental Models 152
Tips to Choose the Right Mental Model 153
Relevance.. 154
Clarity.. 154
Variety and Conformity 155
Know What the Truth Is.............................. 156
Understand the Pros and Cons of Each Model................. 156
Chapter 10: Mental Models Toolbox 158
Artist: What if Creativity Took Precedence 159
Entrepreneur: Rapid Prototyping....................................160
Doctors; Using Symptoms... 161
Journalist: Fact-Checking.. 162
Accountant: Ratio Analysis 162
Final Thoughts 164
References 171

Introduction

We are often faced with the challenge of learning how to become better decision-makers. Perhaps, this is one of the main reasons why you are reading this book. Well, you are not alone. Growing to become a better decision-maker is not something that you can achieve in several minutes or hours. It's a lifelong journey. It takes time for you to learn and master the idea of enhancing your thought processes. Maybe you are racking your brains trying to conceptualize what "mental models" mean. Before defining what "mental models" means, let's take some time to consider why scholars often argue that two heads are better than one.

Indeed, this is something that people have lived to acknowledge and that it has defined how they interact with others. When debating something with other people, the higher the number of folks debating the better. This is because there is a good chance that a solid decision will be made based on different thoughts, assumptions, and experiences brought together. The fact is that when people are taken individually, they are limited by their own experiences. It is for this very reason that we usually conclude that two heads are better than one.

Now, the varying areas of expertise that people boast of leads to "mental models." Interestingly, these are assets that we all have, but we often fail to realize it. The way we think is usually a product of the views and perceptions that we have in our community. People don't think out of concepts that they have invented on their own. Instead, our thoughts are shaped by shared views, norms and perceptions of our community. These shared views provide people with a way of understanding the world around them. Accordingly, you will rarely find folks questioning shared views that are accepted by the majority.

A good example of how mental models are formulated is through the perception that parents should provide mental stimulation to their kids. In this case, most societies will expect parents to play their role by taking good care of their children. Therefore, this is a world view and can be identified as a "mental model." Using this example, people tend to relate with each other peacefully based on such similar views. For you to make better decisions, it is imperative that you comprehend what other people think. Arguably, your behaviors will be celebrated in society only if you conform to the shared views.

When people express empathy toward each other, it shows that they understand each other better. In a way, empathy shows that people not only understand how you are from the outside, but they empathize with how you feel from the inside. Therefore, it goes beyond knowing what a certain individual expects from you. Mental models give you the opportunity to comprehend people's thought processes and their deepest motivations. In addition, the models also give you insight into the emotional landscape that people are operating on. For that reason, with your mental models, you are better placed to make sound decisions.

So, what are mental models? Simply put, these are thought processes that people use in examining problems at hand.[1] It can also be defined as a depiction of the human mind's thought process. Through these models, people can effectively reason. The views, perceptions and imaginations that they have in their minds influence their reasoning. As such, with the right

---

[1] "Mental Models: The Ultimate Guide - HubSpot Blog." 13 Sep. 2018, https://blog.hubspot.com/marketing/mental-models. Accessed 12 Aug. 2019.

mental models, people can make logical decisions that affect their lives positively.

From the mental models that people have, they can define the world around them. They can relate and share ideas with others as a way of improving their lives. Consequently, the absence of mental models in this world would only hinder people from making decisions that affect their lives. What's more, without shared views and mental models, it would be hopeless for people to find collective solutions to their problems. This means that people will not understand each other, as there is nothing that brings them together.

Looking at the bigger picture, mental models not only helps people in understanding how the world works, but it also draws people to comprehend their position in it. It is worth noting that different societies have got varying mental models. Some people might depend on mental models that are destructive. Others might choose to hold on to contradictory models, and they will use them to explain how they view the world.

Mental models matter a great deal. As such, they should not be taken for granted because they influence how people make decisions. Ideally, since life is based on the decisions that we make, it means that mental models play a crucial role in helping us control our lives. This guide aims to help you understand what mental models are and how they can help in transforming your life. You might have been struggling in your life, trying to make sound decisions, but nothing seemed to work. Likewise, it could be that you are trying to take on a new journey where you strive to find direction in your life. This book details the power of mental models and their relevance in critical thinking. Accordingly, through the detailed information you will be getting herein, you will live to become a better version of yourself.

Chapter 1: The Power of Mental Models

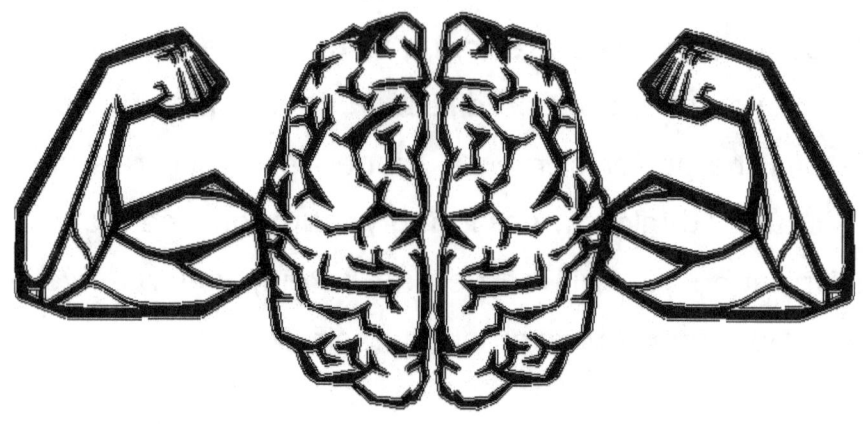

There is no doubt that the view you have about the world around you can have an impact on how life unfolds itself. For people to grow and live happy lives, they have to master the art of creating and adopting the right images in their minds. Ultimately, the images that we develop help to shape the lives that we yearn to live while at the same time limiting us from experiencing harsh life events caused by the poor decisions that we make. This chapter will take you through an in-depth look into what mental models are and how they can affect your life.

Defining Mental Models

Simply put, mental models refers to the way people view or interpret the world around them.[2] Based on the experiences and the societies that we have been raised in, people have varying perceptions and interpretations of this world. The mental models that people have in their minds help them to evaluate what is going on around them and make relevant decisions. There are several notable characteristics that are evident in a mental model.

- Interprets

First, a mental model provides an interpretation of what has been seen or observed. These include events, circumstances, people, and relationships that people have been through. In this regard, mental models will give people the assumption that things, events or circumstances are objective reality. The observations made are not facts, but they are just stories that have

---

[2]"The Role and Power of Mental Models - Integral Leadership Review." http://integralleadershipreview.com/11428-role-power-mental-models/. Accessed 12 Aug. 2019.

been developed based on our understanding of the world around us.

- Disguises

Secondly, mental models disguise the interpretations that we have and it makes us believe that it's the truthful reality. This is done by providing us with justifications and shared views that we tend to believe they are true.

- Determines

In line with the perceptions that we have in our minds, mental models determine possible occurrences as a result of what we choose to believe.

- Dictates

More importantly, mental models dictate the behaviors and attitudes that we adopt following the interpretations that we make. So, this shows that mental models have a direct impact on our lives. Depending on the attitude that one will be taking, they could either choose to view life from a positive or a negative perspective.

Mental models can be applied to our everyday lives. Whether in business, psychology or in the technological world, these models help us to better understand the world around us. It is through the theoretical and practical knowledge gained from these models that individuals can explain the way they are living. For instance, in the world of business, mental models are helpful as they define how people strive to shop economically. Likewise, investors have to comprehend mental models held by their consumers to effectively meet their demands.

Before making any decisions, people reflect on their mental models. Let's take an ordinary example of a man buying flowers for their spouse on Valentine's day. When heading to the store, he will have a specific budget in mind. Chances are he would want to stick to his budget due to other expenses that he might incur on his way home. However, on arriving at the flower shop, the man notices a bigger bouquet that is more appealing than what he had in mind. He decides to purchase the bigger bouquet because at the back of his mind, he understands that his wife will be more delighted. Therefore, in this scenario, the man makes a decision that is influenced by his mental model. The mental model here is based on his knowledge and understanding.

Focusing on the Process, Not the Outcome

In relation to the example provided, it is clear that the decisions you make will have an impact on your life. If you improve your decision making, there is a good chance that you will also enhance the quality of your life. The idea here is that we are not looking at the outcome of your decisions. Rather, the emphasis is placed on the process that leads to good decisions being made.

Interestingly, most people don't look at things from this angle. For people to consider a good decision as "good," they only reflect on the outcome first. So, if the outcome is not desirable, then they end up concluding that a particular decision was bad. An in-depth look into this shows that it doesn't make any sense. The society that we live in is accustomed to the idea of only celebrating folks who succeed. People never take the time to look at the process that other people went through which led to their unpredicted failures.

Often, people perceive mistakes from a negative perspective. What they don't realize is that no one plans to make these mistakes. They happen without people's expectations. As such, individuals should view mistakes as inescapable events that had to occur. This means that making mistakes should not be considered as failing.

Take an example of the famous Titanic ship. Individuals who made the mistakes that led to the sinking of the ship never expected the worst to happen. Before the unforgettable events occurred, they were certain that they had designed the best ship in the world. Therefore, it is only after mistakes lead to bad decisions that people end up regretting.

The reality of the matter is that there are instances when good decisions can lead to unwanted outcomes. Indeed, you can't always be sure that good decisions can make you succeed in life. Most people have made the right decisions only to end with the worst of outcomes. In this regard, success doesn't have to be linked with good decision-making. It should also be seen that good decision-making can lead to success.

With this in mind, ideal mental models require that you focus on the process and not the outcome. Sadly, this is the last thing that people think about every time they are about to make decisions. In most cases, individuals tend to focus more on the outcomes of their decisions and this hinders them from making the right decisions. It is not uncommon for people to fill their minds with doubts before deciding to do anything. If you asked a friend to help you decide on a particular issue, they will jump to ask you, "what will happen if you do this/that?"

Without a doubt, this is the wrong model to use with regard to decision-making. The best move to take should be to pay attention to the process and less on the outcome. There are numerous reasons why people will be blinded to focus on just the outcome. For instance, some might claim that they don't have time, whereas others would blame their lack of knowledge. However, it doesn't matter what your reasons are for failing to concentrate on the decision-making process. The result is that you will end up becoming a poor decision-maker despite of the outcome.

Still on good and bad decisions, it is important to reflect on some of the reasons why most people end up making the wrong decisions.

We Are Sometimes Gullible

Sure, we all like to conclude that we are rational and that we can easily make decisions without being biased. However, this is not the case for most of us. Numerous instances increase the chances of acting irrationally. For instance, when rushing, interrupted, tired, under pressure, etc. These situations could have a negative impact on the decisions that we make. In the end, we find ourselves making the wrong decisions.

Using the Wrong Model

Similarly, using the wrong model could have an impact on the decisions that we make. In this regard, the wrong model will often lead to bad decisions being made. Incorrect interpretations of what is going on around us will often blind us from realizing that we are making mistakes. When people are inexperienced in certain areas, they find themselves in situations where they use less useful models. Therefore, this is what leads them to make the wrong decisions.

Failing to Learn

From what we've discussed about focusing on the process and not the outcome, it is clear that we all make mistakes. The difference is how we perceive them. Failing to learn from these mistakes will only drive us to make similar mistakes repeatedly.

Having the Wrong Information

Wrong or erroneous information will also influence people to make incorrect assumptions about events, things, relationships or people around them.

The reality that we have to deal with is that most people struggle to make the right decision. It's simple, but not easy. If people took the time to understand the world, things would have been different. Unfortunately, most individuals view the world from their own perspectives. Ultimately, this influences their decision-making process as they end up settling for the wrong mental models. Understanding the word just as it is will transform your perspective toward life. You will begin to feel a sense of belonging and enhance your decision-making process.

The more you make sound decisions, the more you will realize that you have plenty of time to yourself. You will free yourself from stress and have more time to enjoy with family and friends. So, how do you understand the world in a way that will help you become a better person?

Understanding the World

It is important to stress the fact that your thoughts are determined by the mental models that you're using. When thinking about budgeting for your groceries, you're using a mental model. When thinking about how the economy works, you're using a mental model. The mind creates the best path that leads us to understand a particular concept in the most simplified manner. For instance, based on our market knowledge, we know that an equilibrium point is reached when the market supply equals the quantity demanded as shown in the figure below.

Figure 1: Market Equilibrium

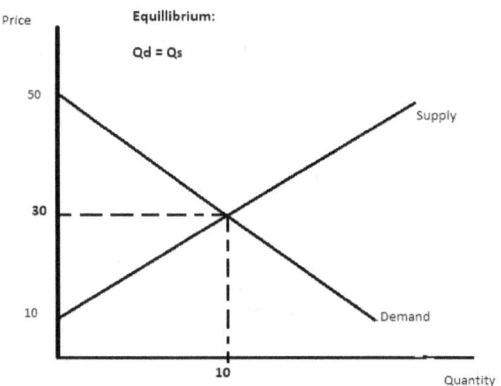

Generally, the mind utilizes existing research models that help us to better understand certain things. Another way of comprehending this is by taking a look at how we segment people based on their personalities. Naturally, people tend to divide themselves based on their perceived personalities. For instance, when hanging out with friends at a party, it is easy to notice how people group themselves. You will find two or three folks in one corner, while others will prefer to stay outside.

In marketing, brands have to communicate with these groups differently since they have varying tastes and preferences. The best brands out there utilize the idea of personality targeting to reach their audiences in the most desirable manner.[3] This form of segmentation is based on Myers-Briggs personality profiling principles. This refers to a questionnaire that groups people based on their personality inventory.[4] According to this profiling tool, there are 16 varying personality types as shown below.

Figure 2: Myers-Briggs Personality Types

ISTJ	ISFJ	INFJ	INTJ
"DOING WHAT SHOULD BE DONE"	"A HIGH SENSE OF DUTY"	"AN INSPIRATION TO OTHERS"	"EVERYTHING HAS ROOM FOR IMPROVEMENT"
Organizer • Compulsive Private • Trustworthy Rules 'n Regs • Practical	Amiable • Works Behind the Scenes Ready to Sacrifice • Accountable Prefers "Doing"	Reflective/Introspective Quietly Caring • Creative Linguistically Gifted • Psychic	Theory Based • Skeptical • "My Way" High Need for Competency Sees World as Chessboard
MOST RESPONSIBLE	MOST LOYAL	MOST CONTEMPLATIVE	MOST INDEPENDENT
ISTP	ISFP	INFP	INTP
"READY TO TRY ANYTHING ONCE"	"SEES MUCH BUT SHARES LITTLE"	"PERFORMING NOBLE SERVICE TO AID SOCIETY"	"A LOVE OF PROBLEM SOLVING"
Very Observant • Cool and Aloof Hands-on Practicality • Unpretentious Ready for what Happens	Warm and Sensitive • Unassuming Short Range Planner • Good Team Member In Touch with Self and Nature	Strict Personal Values Seeks Inner Order/Peace Creative • Non-Directive • Reserved	Challenges others to Think Absent-minded Professor Competency Needs • Socially Cautious
MOST PRAGMATIC	MOST ARTISTIC	MOST IDEALISTIC	MOST CONCEPTUAL
ESTP	ESFP	ENFP	ENTP
"THE ULTIMATE REALIST"	"YOU ONLY GO AROUND ONCE IN LIFE"	"GIVING LIFE AN EXTRA SQUEEZE"	"ONE EXCITING CHALLENGE AFTER ANOTHER"
Unconventional Approach • Fun Gregarious • Lives for Here and Now Good at Problem Solving	Sociable • Spontaneous Loves Surprises • Cuts Red Tape Juggles Multiple Projects/Events Quip Master	People Oriented • Creative Seeks Harmony • Life of Party More Starts than Finishes	Argues Both Sides of a Point to Learn Brinksmanship • Tests the Limits Enthusiastic • New Ideas
MOST SPONTANEOUS	MOST GENEROUS	MOST OPTIMISTIC	MOST INVENTIVE
ESTJ	ESFJ	ENFJ	ENTJ
"LIFE'S ADMINISTRATORS"	"HOST AND HOSTESSES OF THE WORLD"	"SMOOTH TALKING PERSUADER"	"LIFE'S NATURAL LEADERS"
Order and Structure • Sociable Opinionated • Results Driven Producer • Traditional	Gracious • Good Interpersonal Skills Thoughtful • Appropriate Eager to Please	Charismatic • Compassionate Possibilities for People Ignores the Unpleasant • Idealistic	Visionary • Gregarious • Argumentative Systems Planners • Takes Charge Low Tolerance for Incompetency
MOST HARD CHARGING	MOST HARMONIZING	MOST PERSUASIVE	MOST COMMANDING

---

[3]"Intro to Myers-Briggs Personality Types - Referral SaaSquatch." 27 Sep. 2016, https://www.referralsaasquatch.com/myers-briggs-personality-types/. Accessed 13 Aug. 2019.

[4]"Intro to Myers-Briggs Personality Types - Referral SaaSquatch."

Source:"Intro to Myers-Briggs Personality Types - Referral SaaSquatch." [5]

Now, using the Myers-Briggs profiling tool, the idea of categorizing people based on their personalities is made easier. This means that people can communicate effectively since they understand each other better. Why? This is because we are obliged to use a better mental model which provides us with a better grasp of how people behave. For instance, using the frameworks provided above, if you were an ESFP type, it shows that you are most generous. When interacting with an ENTJ type, you will have to approach them in a particular way simply because they are the most commanding.

In an ordinary situation where one is using their own crafted mental models, it would be a daunting task to understand people. We would struggle to try to find shared views that help us to judge people. The point here is that our personal experiences or understanding lack the depth that certain research models provide us. What's more, these observations have unimportant

---

[5]"Intro to Myers-Briggs Personality Types - Referral SaaSquatch."

noise that prevents our minds from correctly evaluating between what's essential and what's not.

People should acknowledge the fact that they can't be proficient in everything they do. Accordingly, with the help of well-researched science-based models, we are better placed to make informed decisions. This leaves us with the conclusion that there are many ways we can understand the world. Of course, one of the main strategies would be to equip yourself with knowledge.

A Multidisciplinary Approach

For you to understand the world, you must equip yourself with knowledge. The mind can be compared to a toolbox. To use this toolbox, you have to fill it with the right tools. Additionally, you should know how to use the tools you have. Therefore, with the right tools and expertise on how to utilize them, you can solve many problems. This is how knowledge is important to your life. You will solve faster and gain more control over your life.

The right tools that should occupy space in your mind are the mental models. Getting to a level of higher understanding is not that easy as it requires you to comprehend different models and how best to utilize them.

So why are mental models important in your life? Simply put, mental models help us to circumvent the complexities of this world. There is a lot that we should grasp. Consequently, to save ourselves from the burden of striving to understand everything, we simply choose to rely on mental models.

It goes without saying that the more tools you have in your toolbox, the easier it would be for you to solve problems. Concerning mental models, grasping a variety of these models guarantees that you can effectively handle problems that come your way. This happens because of the variety of mental models you have bestows you with the advantage of perceiving the world from different perspectives.

An economist and a psychologist will have varying views of the world. However, when they are brought together, they will combine their ideas to come up with better solutions. In the same way, when you have an array of mental models at your disposal, you will make informed decisions.

Still, it is worth mentioning that mental models are always changing. Your mental models will be directly influenced by what you learn and the experience that you gain in your life. So, if an individual has never shopped over the internet, they will assume the best way to shop is by shopping at brick and mortar stores. Sooner or later, when they are introduced to the world of online shopping, their mental models will change. They will appreciate the benefits that come with online shopping as compared to traditional stores. Consequently, as you continue learning, expect changes in your mental models.

The power of mental models can, therefore, be explained through the way in which mental models allow you to have varying worldview dimensions. By striving to ensure that your mental models do not limit you to a particular worldview, you will open yourself up to a world full of opportunities. Mastering several mental models gives you the power to make informed decisions, solve problems faster and gain total control of your life. Remember, the point here is not for you to become an expert in a single model. Rather, you ought to be conversant of the most important models. More information about the best models to unravel is discussed in the following chapter.

Chapter 2: Types of Mental Models

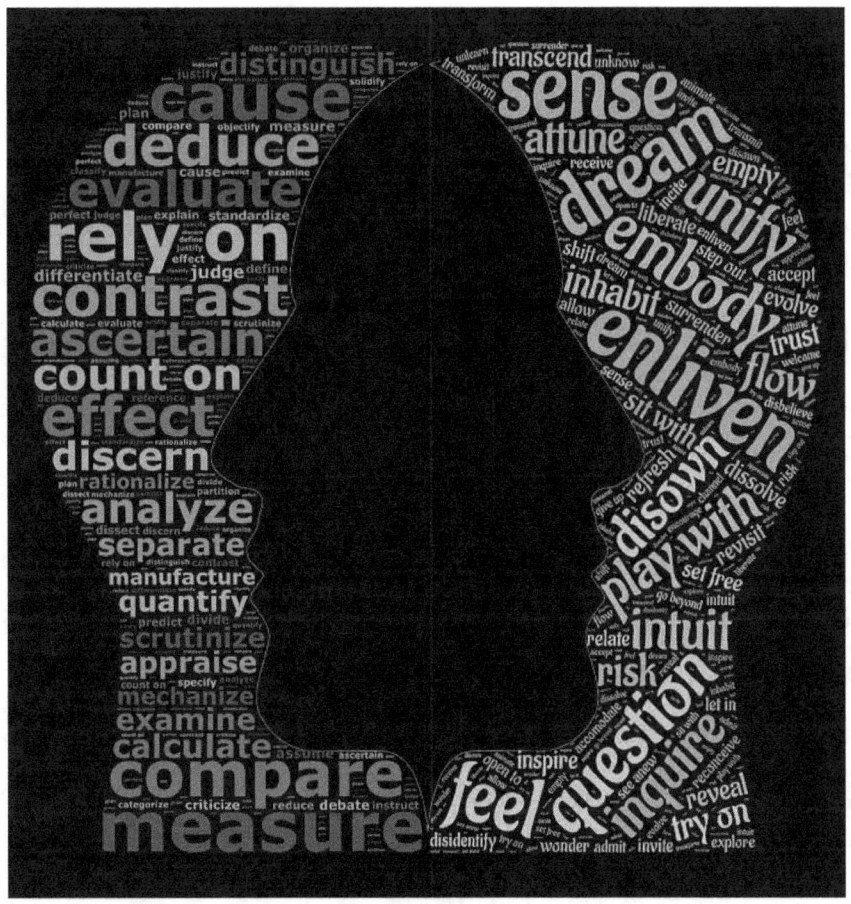

After grasping the basics of mental models and how they can help you to cognize how things work around you, let's dive in to look into the types of models you should grasp. Undeniably, there is a wide array of models that have been formulated throughout history. However, you should realize that you don't have to master all these models for you to improve your thinking skills. Getting a deeper insight into the best models puts you in a good position to master the world around you.

Different mental models that will be discussed in this chapter are from disciples such as chemistry, business, psychology, biology, philosophy, etc. Each disciple has ideal mental models that have been highly ranked over the years.

Comparative Advantage

In the field of economics, comparative advantage is a theory that was introduced by David Ricardo in 1817.[6] According to Ricardo, it was possible for two countries trading with each other to mutually benefit if they were producing their goods/services at a lower opportunity cost.[7] To get the idea of how the theory of comparative

---

[6]"The Principles of Comparative Advantage: Why Tiger Woods Shouldn't ...." https://fs.blog/2009/08/should-tiger-woods-mow-his-own-lawn-the-principles-of-comparative-advantage/. Accessed 13 Aug. 2019.

[7]"Comparative Advantage Definition - Investopedia." 25 Jun. 2019,

advantage work, one should clearly understand what opportunity cost means. Basically, opportunity cost refers to the benefits that an individual misses when they choose one alternative over the other.[8]

Economically, a nation would have comparative advantage over another if at all they can produce their goods/services at a lower opportunity cost as compared to other countries. Let's take an ordinary example of two nations with the following labor costs of production.

Table 1: Labor Cost of Production

Country	Cost per Unit in Man Hours
	Product X
A	10
B	14

---

https://www.investopedia.com/terms/c/comparativeadvantage.asp. Accessed 13 Aug. 2019.

[8]"Opportunity Cost Definition - Investopedia." 25 Jun. 2019, https://www.investopedia.com/terms/o/opportunitycost.asp. Accessed 13 Aug. 2019.

Using the above table, the cost of producing product X and Y is lower in country A. This means that there is an absolute advantage enjoyed by country A in producing both commodities. Nevertheless, applying the principle of comparative advantage here, country A would have a comparative advantage if it produced and exported product X. On the other hand, country B would also have a similar advantage by producing and exporting product Y. The point here is that both countries will benefit from trading together. The assumption made here is that the cost ratios should not be equal.

Employing real-life example, let's assume that Christiano Ronaldo wants to mow his lawn. Indeed, Ronaldo is a famous soccer player. He is famous for his speed and skills on the ball. Since we know how fast Ronaldo is, does this imply that he should mow his lawn?

Ricardo's concept of comparative advantage can help us in deciding whether Ronaldo would be best fitted to mow his lawn. Due to Ronaldo's speed, let's assume that it would take him an hour to complete the job. In the same one hour that he spends here, he could alternatively be featured in an advert that earns him $100,000. Conversely, his next-door neighbor, Mark, can get the job done in four hours. In this period, Mark can offer his plumbing services and earn $120.

From the example provided, Ronaldo's opportunity cost is $100,000. By contrast, Mark's opportunity cost is $120. Ronaldo has an absolute advantage over Mark because he can mow his lawn within a short period. Regardless, Mark enjoys comparative advantage in this case due to his lower opportunity cost of $120 as compared to $100,000 for Ronaldo. If these people work together, they will benefit. Therefore, instead of Ronaldo mowing his lawn, the best move would be to hire Mark. For instance, he could offer Mark $200 to do the job. This leaves both of them benefiting from the trade.

Therefore, with the help of a comparative advantage mental model, one could be influenced to invest their time and money wisely. Without a doubt, it would be a bad idea for Christiano Ronaldo to mow his lawn as explained in the example above.

The Pareto Principle

Another notable mental model that can quickly transform how you do things is the Pareto Principle. The mental model earned its name after the celebrated economist called Vilfredo Pareto. According to this principle, 80% of the consequences are as a result of 20% of the causes. As a result, the principle is popularly known as the 80:20 rule.[9] Pareto was inspired to come up with the principle after noticing the uneven relationship between population and wealth. In this case, Pareto noticed that about 80% of the land was owned by only 20% of the population.[10]

The principle is applicable in various aspects of our lives. In business, for example, 80% of revenue collected can be attributed to 20% of the customers. Similarly, 80% of the sales generated are from 20% of the salesmen. The same principle applies to your personal life. For instance, when you look at your wardrobe, you will notice that you only wear 20% of the clothes you have. Now, consider the number of applications that you have installed on your smartphone. Chances are that 20% of your mobile apps make up for 80% of your daily usage.

---

[9] "Pareto Principle Definition - Investopedia." 19 Jul. 2019, https://www.investopedia.com/terms/p/paretoprinciple.asp. Accessed 13 Aug. 2019.

[10] "Pareto Principle Definition - Investopedia."

So how should the Pareto Principle help in your life? This mental model is handy when it comes to increasing your productivity. Often, people have a difficult time handling their everyday activities. Unfortunately, most individuals go to bed with regrets because they didn't accomplish what they had set their minds to achieve. One of the main reasons why this happens is because there is a lot to do and yet so little time.

With the help of the Pareto Principle, you will learn that your productivity is not evaluated based on the number of activities that you completed. Rather, productivity is determined by the quality of your output. This is to mean that you can do one or two activities a day and still remain productive. Using the Pareto phenomenon, 80% of the results you gain are from 20% of your efforts. Accordingly, mastering the Pareto Principle shows that you will learn how to do more with less.

Of course, this doesn't mean that you should be lazy since you only need 20% of your effort to get optimal results. The point here is that you should learn to prioritize. Prioritizing tasks guarantees that you can do more in little time. At work, for example, getting the most important tasks done first gives you a reason to feel good about yourself. Other unimportant or minor tasks can be delegated to other people. This gives you room to work on what you value most.

Still, you ought to realize that the Pareto Principle cannot be applied to everything you do. Sure, after learning the effectiveness of a new mental model, one would be psyched up to use it everywhere. However, there is a limitation to this. There are instances where 20% of your effort is just not enough to get you the results you need. So, you are required to grind and put a little more effort to get things done. As such, it is worth recognizing when not to apply the Pareto Principle mental model.

Confirmation Bias

We are all raised differently. We have been brought up in distinct environs and this has had a huge impact on what we choose to believe. As a result, any new information that we come across has to be filtered to determine whether we agree or disagree with such notions. When people are choosy on what they prefer to believe, this is termed as confirmation bias. Usually, people make decisions after considering their personal beliefs and experiences. Therefore, some are rigid to accept things that are not part of what they believe to be true.

There is a huge problem faced as a result of the worldviews that we have cemented in our minds. People can be too rigid to accept change. Therefore, individuals will prefer to remain in the same position instead of adopting change in their lives. The resistance to change is what drives people to live in their own bubbles. Arguably, there are numerous instances where we have judged people for failing to see sense in what they are doing. The main issue with confirmation bias is that it clouds our judgment. The worst thing is that you can never realize that you are facing it unless you understand the concept.

Undeniably, we all have friends who would want to reject certain facts even when they are provided with numerical data. This is because the information presented goes against the views that they have. A good example of how confirmation bias affects our choices is in music. People will react differently to conventional forms of music as compared to contemporary music. Our parents and grandparents, for example, they will prefer good oldies songs because it resonates with their upbringing. On the contrary, young people will opt for contemporary music because they believe that it gives them the rush that they desire.

So, how do you protect yourself from confirmation bias? Certainly, this is an important question considering you don't want to live a rebellious lifestyle where you don't agree to share worldviews. The first step to safeguarding yourself against it is understanding the concept of confirmation bias. Regardless, it should be noted that your discerning of the concept will not make you immune to it. We are all humans with faults. As such, don't expect to be perfect.

Maslow's Hierarchy of Needs

Maslow's hierarchy of needs is a concept that was introduced by psychologist Abraham Maslow.[11] According to Maslow, people are more motivated to meet their basic needs as compared to other needs such as safety, self-esteem and self-actualization.[12] With the help of this mental model, people can garner a firm grasp on what motivates people. This theory postulates

---

[11]"Maslow's Hierarchy of Needs - The Peak ...." http://thepeakperformancecenter.com/educational-learning/learning/principles-of-learning/maslows-hierarchy-needs/. Accessed 13 Aug. 2019.

[12]"The 5 Levels of Maslow's Hierarchy of ...." 21 Jul. 2019, https://www.verywellmind.com/what-is-maslows-hierarchy-of-needs-4136760. Accessed 13 Aug. 2019.

that people are self-driven because they yearn to meet particular needs. The model is as depicted in the figure below.

Figure 3: Maslow's Hierarchy of Needs

Source: "Maslow's Hierarchy of Needs vs. The Max Neef Model of Human Scale ...."[13]

---

[13]"Maslow's Hierarchy of Needs vs. The Max Neef Model of Human Scale ...."
https://medium.com/@hwabtnoname/maslow-s-hierarchy-

Maslow's concept is often depicted in a pyramid with the lowest sections showing the most basic needs that will motivate people. Higher levels of the pyramid indicate complex needs. Naturally, people will strive to meet their psychological needs before doing anything else. These needs include food, water, sex, sleep, etc.

The second level of Maslow's pyramid from the bottom indicates safety needs. In reality, this need is more complex as compared to food and water. People desire to live in safe environments. As such, they will work hard to make sure that they are financially stable. Similarly, their safety also touches on their motivation to live healthy lives. As people work to meet these needs, they push themselves to adopt certain behaviors. For instance, they look for jobs, save their money and shift to safe neighborhoods.

On the third tier, you will find love/belonging. This level features social needs such as the desire to be loved and accepted. Here, human behavior is mainly motivated by emotional relationships. For people to meet their social needs they want to have friends and family around

---

of-needs-vs-the-max-neef-model-of-human-scale-development-9ebebeabb215. Accessed 13 Aug. 2019.

them. In addition, they will want to be associated with other social groups in their community. Bearing this in mind, meeting these needs helps people to avoid common social problems such as anxiety, depression, and loneliness.

The next level in the hierarchy shows esteem needs. Maslow pointed out that people look for respect and admiration. Once people have met their basic and social needs, self-esteem desires begin to take shape. For that reason, people will want their individual efforts recognized and appreciated.

At the top level of the pyramid lies self-actualization needs. These are the needs where people aspire to be the best in their worlds. Accordingly, this need is met when people utilize their talents or any potential at their disposal.

Recognizing that people are motivated by different needs can help us to understand why they choose to behave in a certain way. For instance, some folks will be motivated to meet their love needs. As such, we can learn how to relate to them desirably.

Parkinson's Law

Parkinson's law states that "work expands to fill the time available for its completion."[14] This law was framed by Cyril Northcote Parkinson, a celebrated British author and historian. What this law tries to tell us is that if work was meant to be completed in a week, then it will be completed in a week. In this regard, people plan their deadlines based on the time that they have.

Interestingly, this is what happens to most people when they have tasks to complete. If they have ample time to complete activities, they will procrastinate until the last minute. This is a habit that most people develop forgetting the fact that it has a negative impact on their productivity.

An ideal way of utilizing the mental model is by realizing the effects of allowing deadlines to catch up with you. Usually, this builds pressure on you more so when you have fixed deadlines to beat. Therefore, to be on the safe side, you ought to embrace the idea of incorporating micro-deadlines to your activities. Set small goals that

---

[14]"Parkinson's Law - The Personal MBA." https://personalmba.com/parkinsons-law/. Accessed 13 Aug. 2019.

you can achieve within a short timeframe. Achieving these small goals will keep you motivated on completing a particular project. The best part is that it will help you avoid the urge to procrastinate. So, instead of waiting for deadlines to catch up with you, start now.

10/10/10 Rule

The 10/10/10 method is highly applicable to the decisions that we have to make daily. Without a doubt, there are many instances when we find ourselves perturbed, not knowing the best decision to make. Unfortunately, this leaves us making hasty decisions that we end up regretting. To save you from the dilemma, the 10/10/10 method should be utilized. With this method, people are not only forced to consider the short-term consequences of their actions, but they also reflect on the long-term effects.

The bitter truth concerning decision-making is that people find it easy to make decisions that affect them in the short-term. Frankly, it is easy to decide whether something will benefit you in the next 10 minutes or so. However, a problem arises when people should make decisions that appear less impactful at first, but in the long run are beneficial.

When using the 10/10/10 method to help you make informed decisions, it requires you to ask yourself several questions. These questions are based on how you will feel after 10 minutes, 10 months and 10 years. So, when thinking about going on a trip with friends, you should begin by asking yourself how you will feel 10 minutes after paying for the trip. Of course, you might be skeptical about the whole idea of meeting up with friends and the expenses involved. However, take another moment to consider how you will feel in 10 months after you have spent time with your friends. Unquestionably, there is a good chance that you will feel good about the time you spent to catch up with them after a long time. Likewise, you will want to treasure these beautiful memories in 10 years. So, ultimately, you will decide to go on this trip because you know the value it adds to your life.

If hitting the gym consistently is something that you have been struggling with, the 10/10/10 rule is applicable. This method will motivate you to resist the urge to eat junk. Think about it this way, sure eating junk food will only make you feel good for a short period. After eating a junk meal for 10 minutes, you will feel satisfied. What about 10 in 10 months or 10 years? Will you still have similar attitudes toward such meals? There is a high probability that you will regret eating junk because of the negative effects it has on your body in the long run.

The 10/10/10 rule helps you to make sound decisions without allowing emotions to get the best of you. Sometimes emotions tend to blind us from making the right decisions. Thus, if you can get emotions out of your decision-making process, you will nurture your critical thinking skills. Did you know that this is how Ray Dalio, Warren Buffet, and Charlie Munger manage to succeed in prolonged periods?[15] An important lesson that you can learn from them is never to allow emotions to cloud your judgment. With the 10/10/10 mental model, this is possible.

Regret Minimization Framework

The interesting thing about mental models is that even people who seem to have achieved their self-actualization use them. Jeff Preston Bezos, the founder of Amazon, also struggled with the decision of whether

---

[15]"The 10/10/10 Method: Make Decisions Like Warren Buffett and Ray ...." 10 Oct. 2017, https://medium.com/personal-growth/the-10-10-10-method-make-decisions-like-warren-buffett-and-ray-dalio-99e4857d05e3. Accessed 13 Aug. 2019.

to enter into the business of selling books online. Bezos was not afraid to speak his mind, even to his boss, regarding the decision that he was about to take.

Before making the big leap, he wanted to use a framework that would help him to make effective decisions. As a result, he came up with what he termed as the regret minimization framework.[16] This framework is based on the idea that you should project yourself in a certain number of years and picture whether you will regret the decision or not. The mental model can be illustrated using the following figure.

Figure 4: The Regret Minimization Framework

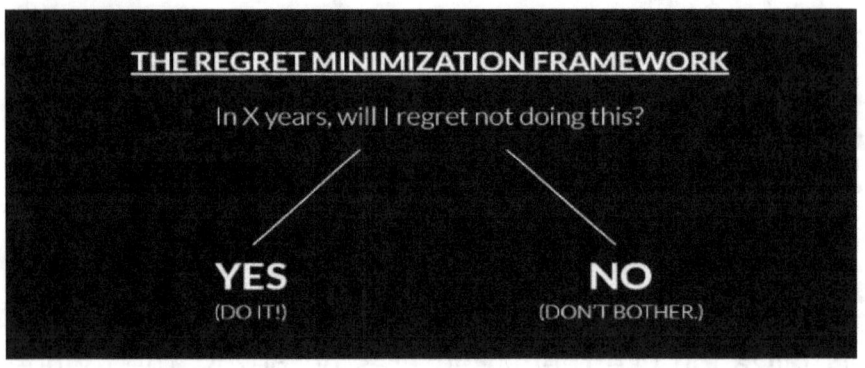

---

[16] "3 Decision-Making Models Used by Warren Buffett and Jeff Bezos | Inc ...." 8 Jun. 2017, https://www.inc.com/sean-kim/how-warren-buffett-and-jeff-bezos-make-smarter-decisions.html. Accessed 13 Aug. 2019.

Source: "The Regret Minimization Framework: How Jeff Bezos Made Decisions."[17]

When using this model, if you think that you will regret not doing something after a certain period, then you should do it without hesitation. On the contrary, if you think that you will not regret not making that decision, then you shouldn't waste time doing it.

Bezos used the model to decide whether or not to start Amazon. He pictured himself 80 years after making the decision that he was about to make. Since he thought that his move would be a big deal, he convinced himself that he was not going to regret starting a company that is now regarded as one of the best in the global marketplace.[18]

Building on this mental model, Bezos found it easier to make the jump. Likewise, you can use the framework to

---

[17]"The Regret Minimization Framework: How Jeff Bezos Made Decisions." https://medium.com/@alyjuma/the-regret-minimization-framework-how-jeff-bezos-made-decisions-4d5a86deaf24. Accessed 13 Aug. 2019.

[18]"Amazon Hits $1,000,000,000,000 in Value, Following Apple - The ...." 4 Sep. 2018, https://www.nytimes.com/2018/09/04/technology/amazon-stock-price-1-trillion-value.html. Accessed 13 Aug. 2019.

look yourself into the future before making any decisions. Thinking long-term allows you to override any doubts that you might have now. If Bezos did it, you can also make a difference in your life using this framework.

Eisenhower Matrix

The Eisenhower Matrix was introduced by Dwight D. Eisenhower. This is an effective time management mental model that was used by Eisenhower during his sensational career. He is best known for being the 34th President of the United States. Eisenhower served two terms beginning in 1953 to 1961.[19] His immense success was attributed to the Eisenhower Matrix box that he often used to manage tasks and time. With this model, one can effectively handle what should be done at the right time.

Eisenhower once pointed out that "What is important is seldom urgent and what is urgent is seldom important."[20] In line with his quote, effective time

---

[19]"Eisenhower Box - James Clear." https://jamesclear.com/eisenhower-box. Accessed 13 Aug. 2019.

[20]"Quote by Dwight D. Eisenhower: "What is important is seldom urgent ...."

management centers around knowing how to differentiate between important tasks and urgent tasks. The Eisenhower Matrix box is depicted in the following figure.

Figure 5: The Eisenhower Matrix

	Urgent	Not Urgent
Important	DO Do it now.	DECIDE Schedule for another time
Not Important	DELEGATE Who can do it for you?	DELETE Eliminate it

Source: "Eisenhower Box - James Clear."[21]

Based on the illustration provided, when using the Eisenhower matrix, you should start by classifying your tasks according to their urgency and importance. In this regard, tasks that are urgent and important should be handled immediately. Important, but not urgent tasks can be scheduled to be done at a later period. Tasks that

---

https://www.goodreads.com/quotes/1161776-what-is-important-is-seldom-urgent-and-what-is-urgent. Accessed 13 Aug. 2019.

[21]"Eisenhower Box - James Clear."

are urgent, but unimportant, can be delegated. Other people who have the right skills for the job can work on these assignments. Lastly, tasks that are neither urgent nor important should be eliminated.

Circle of Competence

The circle of competence mental model is attributed to Charlie Munger and Warren Buffett.[22] Just as the name suggests, this mental model helps investors to identify their circle of competence and stick within it. With regard to financial investments, Buffett uses this model to help him stay within a particular area where he knows that he is an expert. Ideally, the strategy behind this mental model is simple. You only need to focus on a particular area where you feel that you are naturally strong.

As people go through their daily endeavors, they gain experience in what they choose to do or observe. The knowledge that they gain in these areas makes them proficient. As such, according to Buffett, it is best to stick

---

[22]"Finding Your Own Circle of Competence: The Difference ... - Drift." 17 Jun. 2019, https://www.drift.com/blog/circle-of-competence/. Accessed 14 Aug. 2019.

around these areas since it is defined as your circle of competence.

Without a doubt, this mental model makes a lot of sense. Sometimes we find ourselves struggling in areas where we are less skilled or competent. This leaves us with plenty of questions since we don't actually know what we are doing. Instead, we rely on other people to help us maneuver through the challenges we face. Instead of going through such a nightmare, why don't you focus on your circle of competence?

The same strategy can be applied when choosing the right partners to work with. There are people we find it easy to sync with them since we have worked together for years. Partnering with them in other businesses that you are planning to establish is the best bet you can take.

Second-Order Thinking

Decision-making is never an easy task. Often, we find ourselves confused about what we should do about a particular matter. The worst thing is that sometimes we decide to do something, only to cause more problems in our lives. You shouldn't regret this since you cannot predict the future. Therefore, mistakes can happen to anyone. Sadly, it is an unpleasant experience when you keep making mistakes that only deter you from living a happy life.

The second-order thinking model takes into consideration the notion that people should take time to reflect on the long-term consequences of doing something. Normally, people will strive to find quick solutions to their problems. Ideally, this is how the mind is inclined to solving problems. For instance, the immediate action that one would take when they are feeling hungry is to snack on something.

With second-order thinking, you allow yourself to look into a particular decision even before you decide to make it. Before doing something, you will want to ask yourself, "And then what?" What will you gain or lose after making a certain decision? Using the example above, before snacking on anything, you will mull over the aftermath effects of your decision. In this case, if you choose to snack on an unhealthy diet, you will think about the repeated effect of your action. Developing a habit of eating unhealthy dishes repeatedly will affect your body weight.

Second-order thinking will help you think critically about your decision. This means that you will take the best path that will lead you to success. The framework of the second-order thinking mode is something that can be practiced in your everyday decision-making process. Before doing anything, you should always take a step back and question yourself about the consequences of your actions. Besides considering the immediate outcomes, look into the near future. What will happen in a month or two after deciding to do something? This mental model will improve your ability to think critically.

Probabilistic Thinking

The probabilistic thinking mental model focuses on the notion of trying to estimate the likelihood of an outcome occurring. We all desire to make accurate decisions. Doing this guarantees that you transform your life based on the good decisions that you will be making. Honestly, the future is always unpredictable. Accordingly, this is the main reason why the probability theory is considered useful. It allows you to predict your future using different variables that you might go through.

Today, we live in a competitive environment where people no longer struggle to survive. Quite the opposite, people compete to succeed. They desire to be the best in their worlds. Therefore, this demands that they should make the right decisions that lead them to success. The idea behind probabilistic thinking is that you determine the likelihood of something occurring dependent on what you are about to do. If high chances favor the fact that you might fail, then it is prudent to do something else. On the other hand, if chances favor the fact that you could succeed, then you should not hesitate to make a move. After all, we live in an uncertain world. Therefore, the best that you can do is to take the chances that come your way.

Inversion

Charlie Munger once argued that "All I want to know is where I'm going to die so I'll never go there."[23] Perhaps this is the best way of understanding how to apply the inversion mental model. The idea here is that instead of focusing your thoughts on how to solve a certain problem, you could focus on the decisions that you can

---

[23] "Charles T. Munger Quotes (Author of Poor Charlie's ... - Goodreads."
https://www.goodreads.com/author/quotes/236437.Charles_T_Munger. Accessed 14 Aug. 2019.

make to prevent you from solving the problem. Simply put, when thinking about how you can succeed in life, you can opt to invert your thoughts. In this case, you should think about all the things that you can do to prevent yourself from succeeding.

Picture a scenario where you are stuck somewhere. Instead of thinking about how you will get home, think about what you can do to prevent yourself from arriving home. Flipping your problem this way gives you a chance to identify possible obstacles that can prevent you from reaching your goal.

In the real world, when looking to welcome good relationships your way, the best thing that you can do is to stay away from toxic people. So, instead of paying too much attention to finding the right people to interact with, simply avoid toxic individuals. Sounds simple, right?

However, it should be noted that sometimes inverting your problems will not solve them. Nonetheless, it will help you stay away from trouble.

The Map is Not the Territory

We have all used maps at one point in our lives. The basic thing that we understand about maps is that they are a mere abstraction of reality. They are not the reality of what the actual land looks like. So the map is not the territory. This mental model was introduced by Alfred Korzybski, a mathematician, in 1931.[24] There are certain limitations that a map has. The mere fact that it represents a reduction of the actual territory means that other important details are missing. That's not all, to understand a map, it requires interpretation. This paves the way for mistakes. Another flaw in a map is that it could represent a territory that has already changed.

When you think about this model critically, you will understand that the perceptions you have in your mind are not the reality of how things are. Your mind can take you on a wild ride and create maps of reality. This means that if you believe that these perceptions are true, you stand to suffer.

---

[24]"The Map is Not the Territory: How to Improve Your ... - Patrik Edblad." http://patrikedblad.com/mental-models/the-map-is-not-the-territory/. Accessed 14 Aug. 2019.

You will create problems for yourself simply because we are inclined to believe what we think is in line with our beliefs. Therefore, by creating maps of reality within ourselves, we distort our minds from accepting reality. In the end you will make decisions based on your perceptions and not reality.

The best thing that you can do is to treat maps just as maps. They are not reality in any way. Therefore, they shouldn't define how you think. Using this mental model, you should realize that your perceptions are just mere perceptions and nothing more. Recognize them and learn how to effectively see things as they are.

Evidently, from the discussion of mental models, there are plenty of models that you can use to supercharge your thinking. The best part is that you don't have to focus on mastering one single model. Instead, you should strive to understand how each works to help you think critically. One mental model can supercharge others. This is to mean that your understanding of a particular model can help you gain a firm grasp of how you should think and live your life. In line with this, you shouldn't be rigid to change. Try your level best to find your circle of competence and stick within it.

Successful people are using these models to make their lives easier. This is because they understand that we live in an uncertain world. As a result, the best way of reducing this complexity is by relying on mental models to help you cognize how you should think.

Chapter 3: The Role of Mental Models

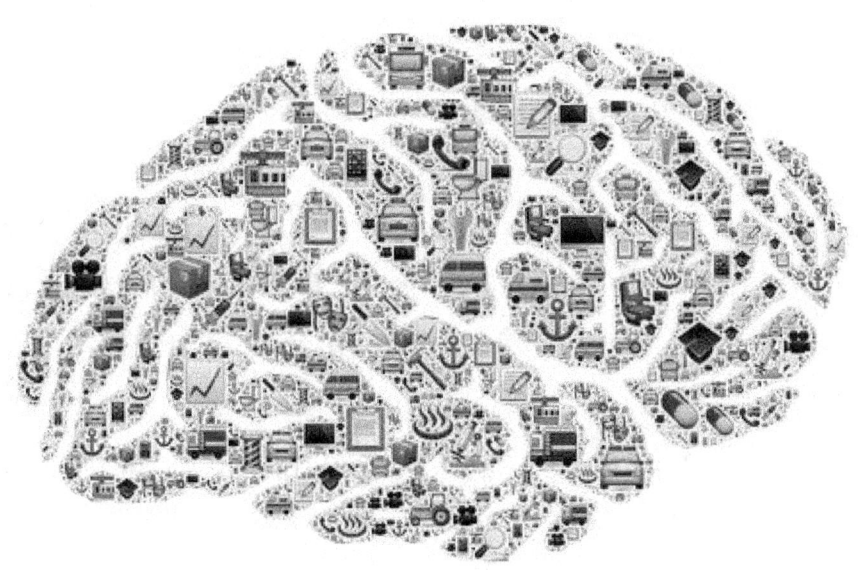

After looking into some of the best mental models you can find, it is imperative to delve into the role of these mental models. Certainly, this is something that might have crossed your mind as you wonder how the models will help you. So, why mental models? What makes these models relevant in your life? Of course, you now know that mental models allow you to understand how this world works. The varying models outlined in the preceding chapter provide you with clear-cut information on comprehending how different thought processes can boost your thinking capacity.

However, it is still worthwhile to question yourself why and how these models can have a positive impact on how you think and perceive the world around you. Looking at the array of mental models that we discussed in chapter 2, it can be argued that mental models can assist you to solve your problems faster. Challenges are part of our daily lives. This is what people have to go through to achieve their goals whether in the short or long run. To ensure that people achieve their goals, decisions have to be made. Accordingly, mental models come in handy to make the decision-making process easier.

In relation to what has been said, mental models, therefore, can act as guides toward the design of the approach you will be taking to handle a particular situation. In business, it will help you and your team to settle for an optimal strategy to solve a problem. The same can be said of your relationships. If there are problems you are facing, mental models can guide you on the best approach to take.

When Jeff Bezos was in a dilemma as to whether to start Amazon, he looked for a framework that would guide him to make the right decision. As such, he came up with the regret minimization framework. Using this framework, he pictured how he would feel in the future depending on the decision he made. In this case, he had a good feeling about starting Amazon and he was sure he would not regret the decision to quit his job and start the company. Therefore, his model provided him with the motivation he needed to easily and effectively make a sound decision.

From Bezos's example, there are three things that we can notice here. First, the regret minimization framework he used gave him confidence in the design he was using. He had the courage to make a big leap to start Amazon. You should bear in mind that he was a senior vice-president at the company that he left.[25] So, he was not quitting because he was not earning well. For that reason, quitting his job was not easy. Without confidence, this is something that he would have just brushed off.

---

[25] "Jeff Bezos Quit His Job at 30 to Launch Amazon--Here Are the 3 ...." 27 Mar. 2018, https://www.inc.com/darren-marble/jeff-bezos-quit-his-job-at-30-to-launch-amazon-heres-how-to-know-if-its-right-time-for-your-big-move.html. Accessed 14 Aug. 2019.

Secondly, the framework that Bezos used provided him with clarity. After coming up with his model, it was now clear that he would regret not implementing what he had in mind. The framework gave him a reason to understand that this was the right direction to take.

Third, Bezos's framework was rooted in the idea of focusing on the long-term consequences of a particular decision. He envisaged himself 80 years after starting Amazon, and he was sure that he would regret if he didn't work on his vision. Clearly, his mental model gave him a reason to believe in the continuity of his strategy.

Therefore, the advantages of using mental models in your life can be summed up as follows. It helps you gain:

- Confidence in your approach

- Clarity in direction

- Continuity of strategy

Confidence in Your Approach

We live in a world full of uncertainty. You can never be sure about anything that you want to do. However, this doesn't mean that there is nothing that you can do to make your decision-making process simpler. Using mental models gives you confidence that the approach you are using has been proven and tested by other successful people in the society. Once your mind acknowledges the fact that your framework is based on solid research, you will have the energy to pursue that which you have been thinking of. This is because you are more convinced that it will work. You have solid proof and nothing can stop you.

Besides, if you are working with a team, the mental models that you use allow them to believe the approach that you plan to use. In a way, when they comprehend how your approach works, they will grasp your understanding of the solution and embrace it.

Leverage Luck and Intent

Since we agree that the world is full of uncertainties, it means that there is room for luck in what we do. Basing our argument on the probabilistic thinking mental model, numerous variables will contribute to succeeding in anything you do. Believe it or not, luck is one of them. The funny thing is that most individuals would want to attribute their success to certain facts. They will give plenty of excuses to justify that the decision they made was accurate. The reality of the matter is that luck influences how we succeed.

When using mental models as a way of improving your thinking abilities, you are more comfortable to open up to the world of possibilities. That's not all, you will also acknowledge the variables that contribute to your success. Simply put, you will embrace the uncertainty that this world puts you through. Accordingly, mental models will be the right tools to steer you in the right direction.

Mental models provide you with the evidence you need to rely on your approach. They are a language that you can read and understand. Language helps you to communicate with other people. It gives you the ability of interacting with others and to know what they feel. In the same manner, mental models are a language that you can master. The good news is that, you will not be the first person to use them. Thousands of people are using these models to solve their problems with ease.

Differentiate Between Solutions

There are varying forms of frameworks that we have looked at in chapter 2. Undeniably, the more you models you grasp, the more informed you will be. For you, it will be easy to distinguish between solutions that can be reached by using these models. At some point, you will realize that there are some models that provide similar solutions. The point here is that models give you the advantage of perceiving this world from different perspectives. Hence, you will not be limited to one solution. You can decide to utilize distinct frameworks to solve the diverse problems you might be facing.

Accept that Ideas Match Needs

Another good thing about mental models is that it provides you with the right platform to confirm that your approach is ideal. In this case, when using any mental model, you will embrace the notion of a higher level of thinking. For instance, prior to making any decision, you will want to compare your decisions to what renowned scholars would do if they were in your situation. Eventually, this puts you in a situation where you make decisions based on what you have validated to be realistic.

Avoid Politics

The confidence that you have in your approach will prevent you from second-guessing. You know what is right and what is wrong. Therefore, you will want to choose the best path with proven track record. Certainly, this is important, more so when working in groups. Some individuals might want to engage in trial and error to solve their problems. With your knowledge and expertise on mental models, this is what you will want to avoid. Making wild guesses on what you should do can easily bring any successful business to the ground. A mental model would save the day as it would provide the best form of interpretation to decide on what you ought to do.

Clarity in Direction

In addition to giving you confidence in your approach, mental models will also provide you with a clear direction on how you should think and act. Throughout your decision making process, you will want to have a clear strategy on how you do things. The people around you should notice that you have a different approach to solving your problems.

Engage in the Whole Experience

There are numerous situations that you will be faced with in regard to decision-making. The problem that you deal with today might not be the same problem that you handle tomorrow. Regardless, if you have mental models to turn to, you will always emerge victorious.

Use Your Approach to Your Advantage

Looking at Maslow's hierarchy of needs model, there is no doubt that people love to feel good about their achievements. Meeting self-esteem and self-actualization needs will give you a reason to be happy about yourself. Mental models will steer you to make the right decisions that impact your life positively. The compounding effect that you will gain from your achievements will boost your self-esteem. Clearly, people will respect you. They will look up to you for assistance whenever they feel stuck. Thus, your sense of direction in life will give you an added advantage as you will accomplish some of your personal needs as argued by Maslow's model.

Transform Yourself

There is an overall transformation that will be taking place in your world. People around you will be the first to notice that you have changed. As you take your time to learn more about mental models, you will advance your knowledge. You will garner a deeper insight on how the world works. Accordingly, it will not be a daunting task for you to make sound decisions.

It is also worth noting that your metamorphosis will be evident through the life's goals that you will be achieving. Indeed, making the right decisions and succeeding in your ambitions go hand in hand. For that reason, you will be glad that things seem to work your way. This is the power of mental models. It delivers you results in remarkable ways.

Continuity of Strategy

A continued use of mental models will provide you with a sense of advancement in how you do things. Besides finding it easy to make decisions and solve problems faster, your new way of thinking will help you gain better control of your life. Most of the decisions that you will be making require you to look into the future. Oftentimes, you will want to consider the long term consequences of your actions instead of just paying attention to short-term gains.

Mental Models Will Help You Change Gradually

At the beginning of this manual, we pointed out that transforming your decision-making process is a lifelong journey. It is not something that you can do overnight. There are numerous mental models that you need to comprehend to become a good decision-maker. The learning process will also not be complete if you fail to put into practice what you learn. Therefore, you must practice the new thinking frameworks that you will be learning from this manual.

Practice makes perfect. You don't have to be an expert in applying mental models to how you think and approach your problems. However, with constant practice, you can polish your critical thinking skills.

Simply put, mental models provide you with the frameworks that you need to make informed decisions in your life. Their role is to bestow you with confidence that your approach toward making certain decisions works. Oftentimes, we are skeptical not knowing the best moves that we should take. This is a common experience more so when faced with big life's decisions. However, with the help of these models, you can understand life from varying perspectives.

To gain the best from these models, you should equip yourself with knowledge by learning how to apply distinct models in the problems that you face. The more you know, the better. We live in a complex world and for you to grasp a solid understanding of how things work, it is vital that you have several mental models in your thinking toolbox.

Chapter 4: Mental Models for Clear Thinking

Every day, our minds are filled with information from everything that is happening around us. As a result, we are left with the challenge of clearing our minds to pave the way for effective thinking. Allowing too much to flow in and out of our minds prevents us from thinking right. The use of mental models can be useful in helping us to think clearly. Most people use these models every day, but they might not realize that they are doing it. When thinking of how you can best relate with your friends and relatives, you are using a mental model. When pondering on how to budget for your monthly expenses, you're also using it.

Any framework used to help you in grasping something easily is perceived as a mental model. Practically, these models can be identified as the apps present in your mind. With the help of each app you have stored in your mind, you can make the right decisions. Also, the more apps you have, the easier it will be to solve the problems in your life. Why? This is because you have a wide array of tools that suit different kinds of problems that you might be going through.

This chapter takes on a specific angle on how mental models can help you think clearly. With the advancement in technology, there is a wide array of devices that can be used to gain access to information. The advent of the internet, for example, has made information available to us whenever we need it. Unfortunately, this flooding of information has been more of a distraction to most individuals out there. Accordingly, mental models are more important than ever before. So, we must learn how they can be used to bring about clarity in how we think.

How to Think Clearly

Clear thinking is not as easy as you might think. It is a challenge that most people have to go through more so when they have to deal with other stressful issues. Your ability to think can also be affected when you're feeling tired and overwhelmed. There are several basic things that you can do to help yourself think clearly. Some of them are succinctly discussed below.

Check Your Attitude

Your ability to think clearly will largely depend on your desires. Often, you will find it easy to sit down and think of the strategies that you can adopt to achieve your goals. Of course, this is dependent on if you have goals. When you don't want to achieve something, it is also easy to think of all the things that you can do not to accomplish this. Therefore, to think clearly, it is imperative to be honest about your goals and ambitions. Is this something that you really want in your life? Ideally, developing the right attitude will be helpful toward bringing clarity in the goals that you wish to attain.

Use Your Passion

There is a good reason why successful people will always advise you to follow your passion. The reality is that you have never heard them tell you to follow your emotions. Your passion toward a particular goal will help you to overcome any challenges associated with it. Passion drains away all the negative thoughts that could deter you from thinking clearly about the task ahead. Conversely, emotions will do just the opposite. Allowing your emotions to get the best of you will only make you feel overwhelmed about what you should do. Usually, you will find yourself focusing more on the obstacles that you must go through. Therefore, to think clearly, it is advisable to use passion to keep your emotions in check.

Use Negative Thinking

It might sound controversial that you should use negative thinking to help you. It is possible. Remember, we are talking about finding the right frameworks to help you understand something better. So it is worthwhile to consider how negative thinking can help clear your mind.

Believe it or not, there is a positive power in negative thinking. When striving to achieve goals, most people will embrace the idea of thinking positively. Certainly, thinking positively works in many ways. It gives your mind a chance to focus your energy on what you can do to ensure you accomplish set goals. Interestingly, negative thinking can help you understand the main reasons why you might not accomplish a particular goal. Therefore, looking at this from a positive perspective, you can take advantage of your negative thinking to bring about positivity.

For instance, consider a scenario where you aspire to work in a competitive industry. If you want to work in one of the best firms in the industry, reflect on some of the reasons why you might not be hired. Some of the reasons that you might list here include your lack of skills in that particular field and your lack of experience. Using these "why not," you can convert them into "how to." Therefore, to effectively land on a good job, you will have to take relevant courses and thereafter gain experience by taking on different jobs. So, if you can tap into the positive power of negative thinking, you can help set your mind to focus on what you want.

Use Cool Logic

Achieving a clear focus you need on what you want to achieve might be easy in the short run. Most people find it easy to concentrate for a few weeks or months before losing track of what they are doing. Therefore, as part of ensuring that you maintain a clear focus on what you desire, you should use a cool logic. How does this work? Cool logic relates to the idea of concentrating on the issue at hand. You should not allow anything else to distract you. For example, if you are working on a project, your mind should concentrate on the project and nothing else. Normally, it is easy to get distracted and allow your ego to control how you think. In this case, you will be withdrawn to think about how you are better than others in doing a particular task. As a result, instead of focusing on the task at hand, you will pay too much attention to competing with your colleagues. Ultimately, this will have a negative impact on the outcome of the project.

Challenge Your Preferences

Several presumptive beliefs could affect the clarity of your thoughts. The ideas that you have developed in your mind about a particular issue can deter you from thinking about anything else. A good number of people will want to settle for the most expensive wines simply because they believe in the notion that the price of the bottle determines how the wine tastes. However, this might not be true if you engage in a blind taste test. You might come across something that you will like. The point here is that you should challenge your preferences by trying something that you have never done before. You will be surprised that you could make informed decisions to the least of your expectations.

Think About Thinking

The aspect of being aware of your thought processes is termed as metacognition.[26] For you to think clearly, you should be aware of how you are thinking. Therefore, you shouldn't allow your thoughts to flow freely without being aware of them. Instead, it is imperative that you plan and assess how you are thinking. The advantage gained through metacognition is that you will enrich your learning experience. For instance, your self-awareness will drive you to think clearly about how to accomplish a particular task.

---

[26]"Metacognition | Center for Teaching | Vanderbilt University." https://cft.vanderbilt.edu/guides-sub-pages/metacognition/. Accessed 15 Aug. 2019.

Ideal Mental Models for Clear Thinking

The tips discussed above will help you free your mind from any thinking challenges that you might be experiencing. You will find it easier to make smart decisions even when faced with difficult situations. However, you can improve on this by learning to use some of the best mental models on clear thinking. Combining the tips with the models that will be detailed here will ensure that you have varying perspectives of looking at any situation that you are faced with. Just to remind you, the more mental models you know, the easier it will be for you to make smart choices.

First Principles Thinking

Some problems appear too complex for us to solve. Without a doubt, this is a dilemma that most people go through in their lives. Well, you shouldn't be stuck when faced with such circumstances because you can apply mental models. An ideal mental model to use here would be the first principles of thinking. This model comes highly recommended when dealing with challenging situations.[27] The best part is that this framework will push you to think for yourself.

The first principles thinking has been there for several years, but it recently became popular in 2002 after Elon Musk stressed on the importance of using it.[28] This framework focuses on the idea that one should think like a scientist. The reason for taking this direction is because scientists don't use assumptions. Their conclusions are often made after facts have been proven.

Theoretically, first principles thinking will require an individual to think critically about a certain situation until they are left with the truths that define the problem they are facing. This is to mean that you shouldn't make decisions like other people. You should mull over thinking deeper. The easiest way of grasping the meaning of this principle is that when faced with a problem, the first thing that you should do is to deconstruct. After that, focus on reconstructing.

---

[27]"First Principles – BJJ Mental Models." https://bjjmentalmodels.com/first-principles/. Accessed 15 Aug. 2019.

[28]"First Principles – BJJ Mental Models."

The first step of deconstructing requires that you ask yourself intelligent questions regarding your situation or problem at hand. Additionally, you should have a deep understanding of frameworks from distinct disciplines. It is crucial that you get more information about varying forms of mental models. Your knowledge is required to guarantee that you can look at your problem from varying perspectives.

Your next move will be to bring together the pieces that you had broken down in the first step. Again, for you to effectively reconstruct, you have to practice how to do it. You could have an idea of how to do something. However, a standalone idea cannot help you to make good decisions. You need to combine several ideas to make valid conclusions. Practicing this more often will strengthen your mental muscles. Eventually, you will improve your thinking skills and end up making sound decisions.

Jeff Bezos used the first principles thinking at the time he established Amazon in 1995. He had two principles that would guide his business to thrive. First, his goal was to focus on the long-term. Secondly, his mission was to focus on the customer instead of the competition.[29] Certainly, with these guiding principles, Bezos managed to drive his company to blossom and become a global market leader.

Thought Experiment

The thought experiment mental model can help you think clearly by solving difficult problems. The thought experiment encourages speculation. What's more, it forces people to alter their paradigms. Instead of reasoning like other people, thought experiment model pushes you out of your comfort zone. As a result, it forces you to ask yourself rhetorical questions that are complex. Through this style of thinking, it unveils the things that you don't know and some of which you know.

The advantage gained in using the thought experiment is that it encourages innovative ideas by pushing you beyond your thinking boundaries. Therefore, you will not be limited to the things that you already know. One major challenge with this mental model is that it appears

---

[29]"Latticework of Mental Models: Thinking From First Principles - Safal ...." 7 Mar. 2018, https://www.safalniveshak.com/latticework-of-mental-models-thinking-from-first-principles/. Accessed 15 Aug. 2019.

impractical. Nevertheless, scholars believe that it can be used theoretically.[30]

BATNA

BATNA is the acronym for Best Alternative To a Negotiated Agreement. This mental model can help you during negotiations. Normally, there are instances when negotiations reach a deadlock. This is a situation whereby parties cannot agree on a particular issue. In such cases, there should be an ideal alternative since parties negotiating cannot agree.

It is worth noting that BATNA should be taken into consideration even before engaging in negotiations. Before entering into negotiations with any individual, you should be aware of your BATNA. The benefit that you gain here is that:

- It gives you the best alternative in case you fail to agree.

- It gives you an upper hand during negotiation since you will have negotiation power.

---

[30]"Mental Models: The Best Way to Make Intelligent Decisions (109 ...." https://fs.blog/mental-models/. Accessed 15 Aug. 2019.

- It helps you dictate your reservation point. This is the lowest price that you can accept in the deal.

Therefore, knowing your BATNA will help you to think clearly when negotiating with people. Going into negotiations without BATNA will only influence you to settle for anything just to close the deal. This is not a smart way of making decisions.

Compounding Knowledge

Compounding knowledge is a mental model rooted in the economic concept of compounding interest. It can be understood as the growth that emerges from your previous growth.[31] The framework is not only applicable in your investments, but it can also be applied to your business, relationships and knowledge.

People are always on the verge of consuming information. What they fail to realize is that most of them consume expiring information. This is something that Warren Buffett strives to steer away from. Instead of focusing on consuming information that is not

---

[31]"How I Live My Life With Mental Models - Jayme Hoffman - Medium." https://medium.com/@jaymehoffman/7-mental-models-i-live-my-life-by-e79742d4f074. Accessed 15 Aug. 2019.

important, Buffett focuses on equipping himself with the knowledge that would help him manage his companies successfully.[32] The idea here is to learn something new that would bring about a positive change in what you do.

Gaining and gathering information from time to time will undeniably lead to compounding benefits. Learning something today and combining it with something else that you learn on the following day will make you a better person. Filling your mind with expiring information that is of less importance is easy, but the reality is that it will not help you in days or months to come.

So, how do you tell that you are consuming expiring information? Information that is marketed to you is not as useful as you might think. Also, if you find that the information lacks meaning and that you can easily consume it, then chances are that the information is not credible. In addition, you will soon realize that it will be irrelevant after a short while. Take, for instance, the habit of watching the news and keeping yourself updated on what is going on around you. Doing this only fills your

---

[32]"Compounding Knowledge - Farnam Street."
https://fs.blog/2019/02/compounding-knowledge/.
Accessed 15 Aug. 2019.

mind with expiring information. Why don't you spend this time garnering knowledge about things that will help you in years to come?

Of course, we are not saying that we should copy the likes of Warren Buffett, but it is important that we acknowledge how these models have helped people to succeed in their lives. Accordingly, there is a lot that we can learn from how they choose to use these models.

Occam's Razor

Occam's Razor is a mental model that is attributed to William of Ockham. He did not introduce the term, but his style of reasoning inspired people to come up with the heuristic.[33] The simplest way of comprehending this concept is that the simplest solution to a particular problem is regarded as correct.

We cannot deny the fact that we always strive to simplify our lives. Everybody does. However, we find ourselves complicating how we live and how we deal with our problems. Interestingly, some billionaires astound us with the way they choose to live their lives. Mark

---

[33]"The Danger of Oversimplification: Use Occam's Razor Without Getting ...." https://fs.blog/2017/05/mental-model-occams-razor/. Accessed 15 Aug. 2019.

Zuckerberg is a good example. It is not uncommon to see him in a gray T-shirt. If you can recall, Steve Jobs also wore his black turtleneck for almost all occasions. This raises eyebrows, right? Indeed, these folks can afford fancy outfits, but they choose to wear similar outfits most of the time.

Using Occam's Razor philosophy, simplicity is the key to success. The idea of wearing similar clothes every day as evidenced by some billionaires is a way of saving themselves time. Without a doubt, knowing that you will wear a gray T-shirt every day can help you save time. Moreover, it can save you brain power that you can use in making informed decisions.[34] The point here is that you should not allow trivial things to distract you from focusing on what is important.

Clearing your mind to help you make the right decisions is not an easy feat. However, it is something that you can manage if you used the tips and mental models discussed herein. One important fact about mental models is that they complement each other. This means

---

[34]"Why Successful People Wear the Same Thing Every Day | Inc.com." 20 Feb. 2018, https://www.inc.com/craig-bloem/this-1-unusual-habit-helped-make-mark-zuckerberg-steve-jobs-dr-dre-successful.html. Accessed 15 Aug. 2019.

that for one mental model to be effective, you have to apply other models in your decision-making. In addition, you should embrace the idea of gaining more knowledge about a particular matter. Don't just limit yourself to one or two models. Strive to gain insights on some of the best that will be continuously discussed throughout this guide.

Chapter 5: Mental Models for Critical Thinking

What is critical thinking? Simply put, this refers to the ability to make a reasoned judgment by effectively analyzing information.[35] Practically, it involves the

---

[35] "Critical Thinking Definition, Skills, and Examples - The Balance Careers."

application of reasoning to determine whether a certain claim is true or not. It is important that you take note that critical thinking doesn't involve the idea of coming up with claims. Rather, it delves more into the evaluation of such claims.

Often, when individuals talk of enhancing their minds, what they focus on is equipping themselves with knowledge and distinguishing the thoughts that they should have. Interestingly, they fail to mull over the way the mind functions. Therefore, when people try to improve how they think, they simply pay attention to what they are thinking about and the information they allow into their minds. This is not the best way of improving the mind. For you to improve how you think, it is crucial that you monitor how you think. In other words, you should think about thinking.

So, how do you know that you are thinking critically? Critical thinking is a sophisticated process. Nonetheless, when you spend time thinking about whether your ideas make sense, then you can argue that you are thinking critically. There are a number of things that you can do

---

https://www.thebalancecareers.com/critical-thinking-definition-with-examples-2063745. Accessed 15 Aug. 2019.

when you are a critical thinker. First, you will find it easy to comprehend logical links between varying ideas. Also, you will solve your problems more systematically. That's not all—you will be in a position to determine the aptness and significance of ideas.

Critical thinking is a skill that can be acquired by almost anyone. However, most people fail to develop the skill due to the misconceptions associated with critical thinking. For instance, a good number of people will conclude that the process is difficult and would give up on it. Therefore, their lack of information about critical thinking and its importance prevents them from gaining interest in the matter.

Some people will argue that critical thinking is a detached process that is cold and unemotional. What these individuals fail to realize is that critical thinking is liberating. When you can think critically you will find yourself resourceful. As such, this is a liberating experience since you will be honing your critical thinking skills from time to time. Other individuals will be discouraged to go through the process due to the assumption that it brings about change. Indeed, critical thinking will help you detach from old assumptions that you might have been holding on to. Accordingly, you will be more informed on the best strategies that you can adopt to make systematic decisions. So, it is not a bad idea if you know what you are getting into.

Components of Critical Thinking

Critical thinking is a process that you have to master. It has several components that define how critical thinking works and how it can help you think critically. The main components of critical thinking are briefly discussed in the following paragraphs.

Perception

People have varying perceptions with regard to the experiences that they go through. Something exciting to one individual might be regarded as less thrilling to another person. Therefore, perception is the way people interpret their observations, ideas, experiences, etc. Your perception will have an impact on how you think. If you are happy about a certain experience, you will think positively about it. On the contrary, if you are not happy, you will have all the reasons to detest a particular activity.

Assumptions

Assumptions also define how you think. They form an integral part of critical thinking. Often, the assumptions that we make are normally implied. Therefore, some people might not notice that they are making assumptions before deciding to do something. It is easy for people to make assumptions because they are comfortable with them. Usually, they are derived from how we perceive the world around us. They are based on our beliefs and how we choose to understand certain concepts.

Emotion

Emotions also evoke thoughts. For that reason, you cannot think without having any emotions. Folks who are critical thinkers have mastered the art of learning how to think without allowing emotions to get in their way. What they do is develop self-awareness. They recognize the presence of these emotions and learn to let go.

Argument

In addition to the above elements, critical thinking also requires you to develop an argument. You will be debating against yourself on whether something is true or not true, valid or not valid. After thinking critically, you should be able to come up with a reasonable argument.

Logic

Logic brings into the picture the aspect of deductive and inductive reasoning. The former relies on hypothesis or general statements. Deductive reasoning pushes you to evaluate the likelihood of reaching a specific goal.[36] On the other hand, inductive reasoning takes into account the observations made and makes broad generalizations. In other words, for you to come up with conclusions, you have to make observations. Both forms of reasoning will transform you into a smart decision-maker.

Understanding Claims, Issues And Arguments

After looking into some of the elements of critical thinking, it is imperative that you grasp how claims, issues and arguments form an important aspect of critical thinking.

---

[36]"Deductive Reasoning vs. Inductive Reasoning | Live Science." 25 Jul. 2017, https://www.livescience.com/21569-deduction-vs-induction.html. Accessed 15 Aug. 2019.

Claims

Depending on the beliefs that people have, they could say something about what they choose to believe. In politics, for example, people will choose to support a particular candidate over the other because of what they believe about the candidate. Therefore, their statements are claims. This is something that a few people will agree to. Claims are the things that people say to express their opinions about a specific matter at hand.[37] Claims are not facts. Thus, they are arguable.

There are different kinds of claims. Some claims are debatable whereas others are simply obvious that they are true or false. This means that some of the claims we make will require careful examination. Others will not because of their obvious nature. Claims concerning the personal decisions that you should be making should be carefully evaluated. For instance, a decision to marry the person that you are dating. Such a claim will demand that you evaluate its viability before doing anything. Additionally, claims that touch on societal issues will also call for a thorough assessment. The government cannot

---

[37]"Argument: Claims, Reasons, Evidence - Department of Communication." https://www.comm.pitt.edu/argument-claims-reasons-evidence. Accessed 15 Aug. 2019.

just decide to provide free healthcare services to its citizens.

Issues

After expressing your views by making claims, you will want to question these claims. For instance, the claim of whether or not to marry the person you are dating can be questioned. Questioning your claim raises an issue. This is where critical thinking comes in. The way you will think to evaluate your claims and come up with a reasonable argument will tell a lot about your critical thinking skills. To solve your issue, this requires you to answer the question raised on your claim. Should you marry or not?

This brings up an argument. However, for your claim to be considered as an argument, you have to provide solid evidence relating to your issue as whether to marry or not. This means that if you lack evidence to support your claim, then it wouldn't call for further examination. For example, your claim will not be debatable if you haven't met the person you intend to marry. It's so obvious that this cannot happen. Therefore, there is no argument about an issue that can't be raised.

Arguments

After raising an issue, the next thing would be to evaluate whether to move toward the left or right. As mentioned earlier, arguments are an integral part of critical thinking. This is the point where you determine whether a claim is true or false, valid or not valid. Usually, people tend to complicate arguments. In the real sense, they are quite simple. Giving out your argument means that you should only provide reasons why you think your claim is valid or not valid depending on what the issue is about. If an individual argues that they should marry because they fell in love, this is just but their argument. To this point, you cannot tell whether their argument is valid.

Determining whether arguments are valid or invalid is what critical thinking is all about. Many things should be taken into consideration before claiming that an argument is good. To ensure that you make sound decisions, critical thinking mental models should help you out. Some of these models are discussed in the following section.

Other Critical Thinking Mental Models

The mental models that will be discussed in this section can be used alongside other models that have been pointed out in this guide.

Ad Hominem

The Ad Hominem mental model is basically a character attack. When in an argument, instead of focusing on the argument, one will focus on discrediting the character of another individual.[38] For instance, one could bring up a good argument about a certain political issue. However, instead of debating on the claim, someone could discredit the individual by claiming that they were once arrested or that they are not worthy of discussing anything. This is something that you might have experienced before. Sometimes people tend to focus on discrediting others as a way of throwing away the reasonable arguments that they might have presented.

---

[38]"Your logical fallacy is ad hominem." https://yourlogicalfallacyis.com/ad-hominem. Accessed 16 Aug. 2019.

Hanlon's Razor

Something that could evoke a chuckle about this world is that people are always thinking that everyone is against them. When something bad happens to us, the first conclusion that we make is that life is against us. When your spouse fails to understand your reasons for not attending a certain event, you will think that they simply want to make you angry. Your neighbor's children playing on your lawn might have you jumping to the conclusion that they just want to ruin your day. The manager is too strict on you, and the first thing that will come to mind is that they are not happy that you are successful. These are the thoughts that we allow to occupy space in our mind. Unfortunately, most of us hold these thoughts to be true and they end up affecting how we feel and think.

The reality is that the explanations that we have in our minds regarding what is happening around are rarely true. Chances are that your manager is strict. This is how they prefer to work. Maybe they also have deadlines to meet. You can't blame them for being strict with you. Hanlon's razor mental model can help you to think critically about what is happening here.

Using the examples above, the explanations that you have in your mind are not adequate to provide you with solid evidence that everything is happening against you. According to Hanlon's razor, one should not attribute malice to things, actions, experiences or people if events can be satisfactorily explained by neglect.[39]

The advantage of using Hanlon's razor mental model in your life is that you will learn how to relate to other people. This is because you will be less judgmental of them. Instead of jumping to conclusions, you will show more empathy toward other people. Hence, you will offer them the benefit of the doubt that they could be right.

Additionally, the same can be applied to business. You will strive to understand the individuals you interact with. As such, you will value the importance of thinking rationally prior to believing any explanations that come to your mind.

One fact that we have to acknowledge is that we spend most of our time interacting with other people. Whether at work or at home, we are always communicating with

---

[39]"Hanlon's Razor: Relax, Not Everything is Out to Get You - Farnam Street." https://fs.blog/2017/04/mental-model-hanlons-razor/. Accessed 16 Aug. 2019.

other people. Therefore, assuming intent from everything that occurs could only make our lives more complex. Honestly, people are always fast to look for other individuals to blame for their misfortunes. You will want to believe that you are poor because of the corruption existing in your country. Also, you will blame your coworkers for submitting their reports on time.

Interestingly, we tend to forget that we have also made such mistakes at one time in our lives. Maybe you are blaming your team for being late. At one point you might also have been late and inconvenienced them. In addition, you can't say that you're perfect. There may have been a time that you failed and disappointed someone. Therefore, before taking out your anger on another individual, you should take a step back and mull over whether your emotions are justified.

To effectively deal with such situations, you should think about educating those who are causing problems in your life. Talk to them about the effects of their actions and inform them about the best way they can behave or act. This way, you will help each other avoid such situations occurring repeatedly.

Surfing or Riding the Wave

This mental model is mostly applicable to business situations. When entering any untapped market, there are plenty of opportunities to take advantage of. The surfing mental model, as used by Charlie Munger, argues that a business should try to maintain its position in the wave to guarantee that they grow.[40] Similar to the surfing sport, if a surfer approaches a wave at the right time, they can surf for long only if they maintain the right position on the wave.

Therefore, this model stresses the importance of taking the best advantage of any situation that comes your way. It doesn't have to be only in business, but you can also apply the model in real-life. This means you should strategically position yourself in a way that you can take full advantage of situations that impact your life positively.

---

[40]"Surfing or "Riding the Wave" – Best Mental Models." 25 Sep. 2018, http://bestmentalmodels.com/2018/09/25/surfing-or-riding-the-wave/. Accessed 16 Aug. 2019.

Illusion of Control

The uncertainties of this world often lead people to make the wrong decisions or simply to give up on what they intended to do. When faced with challenging situations, the best way of dealing with them is by believing that you can. Allowing the perception that you cannot do it only drives you to give up. If you believe that you cannot do it, then most certainly there is nothing that you can do about it.

Unfortunately, the inability to do something about a situation doesn't just end there. There are negative effects that you could experience as a result of the mindset that you have. In this case, you will develop cognitive stress. You will be worked up that you cannot do anything to free yourself from the dilemma that is facing you.

The illusion of control mental model is a framework that can help you to eliminate uncertainty. This means that using this model, you will develop the right mindset that everything is under control. Accordingly, you will have every reason to be optimistic about life.

Developing a sense of control gives you confidence to live your life with energy. You will find it exciting that you are always optimistic about everything regardless of how other people might see it.

The notion of living with certainty shouldn't be taken too far. One thing for sure is that, if we all knew about our futures, life would be boring. We would be forced to live a life without any thrills or surprises. Regardless, it is imperative that you maintain a healthy state of optimism. You should strive to train your mind that everything is under control. Ultimately, you will also gain a better control of your life.

Applying Mental Models in Critical Thinking

After looking at a few mental models that you can use to improve your critical thinking skills, let's consider how you can apply some of the mental models that had been previously discussed.

The Pareto Principle and Critical Thinking

Critical thinking can indeed change your life since you will be making systematic decisions more often. Of course, we can't deny the fact that our decisions affect our lives. When we make the right decisions, it influences the events that happen to us. For instance, deciding whether to marry can transform your life.

Similarly, making the right move to start a business can also change your life completely.

Remarkably, our lives are defined by the activities that we engage in every day. If you choose to sleep every day instead of working, you can be sure that there are no goals that you will be expecting to accomplish. Nevertheless, working more hours in a day also doesn't guarantee that you will be productive. Vilfredo Pareto in his Pareto Principle argued that you can do more with less.

So, how should you use this mental model to think critically about your daily activities? People are often faced with the challenge of shopping for only the things that they need. Have you ever been a victim of impulse buying? Well, we all have. You're walking down the street, you notice something that captures your attention and you buy it without thinking twice. After a day or two, you realize that what you bought is not as important, so you ditch it.

Your wardrobe is true evidence that you have engaged in shopping habits that only take away space from you. According to the Pareto Principle, 20% of your wardrobe account for 80% of what you frequently wear. This means that most of the things that you have are there to occupy space.

The same principle can be applied to your relationships. Sometimes you will want to believe that you have many friends. However, the truth is that you only interact with a few of them. Your call log on your smartphone can show this. There are some people you rarely communicate with and yet you call them friends.

The notion behind the Pareto Principle is that it helps you to understand that you have limited resources to utilize. Therefore, you should learn to prioritize what is important. When thinking about doing certain activities, you should take a step back to consider whether they are important to you. You should dedicate more time to higher priority tasks. Adopting the 80/20 mindset will help you value your time and focus on the most important things first. Ultimately, you will waste little time chasing the wind.

Maslow's Hierarchy of Needs and Critical Thinking

Your critical thinking skills can also be improved by using Maslow's hierarchy of needs. With the help of this model, you will understand how people are motivated with the needs that they ought to accomplish. People will always be driven to achieve their basic needs before anything else. Accordingly, food, water, sleep and other psychological needs will come first. The same motivation will push you to work hard to ensure that your family can eat and sleep.

Applying the Maslow's mental model can help you make smart decisions concerning the needs that you should strive to meet first. Instead of paying too much attention to your self-esteem needs, you will want to put your family first. Therefore, you increase the likelihood of living a happy life full of contentment.

Oftentimes, we have been victims of misplaced priorities. Some people will spend more time focusing on their careers and they forget to spend time with family and friends. In the end, most of them realize that life without love is not as rewarding. We have seen successful people die of depression. Maslow's model can help you comprehend how to balance your needs in life. So, before making hasty decisions on what you should achieve in your life, you should think critically using Maslow's model.

10/10/10 Rule and Critical Thinking

10/10/10 rule can also help you think critically and overcome tough decisions that you might be facing. Say you receive a wonderful job opportunity. This is something that you have been waiting for all this while. Besides giving you more money, the promotion is also a promotion from the current position that you hold. Such opportunities are rare to come by. The first thought that comes to mind is that you should accept the offer without thinking twice.

However, accepting this job means that you will have to relocate. The thought of shifting states tears you apart as you have spent years building what you have now. Your family and friends are here. Your neighbors are people you have interacted with and they have become part of your family. Now, you begin to ask yourself whether you can leave your friends and family behind to build your career.

Moving with your family is also a difficult choice because you will disrupt their lives. They will relocate to different schools and also miss their friends if you will be moving with them. Indeed, this is a tough decision to make and you are not sure what to do. So, should you stay or leave?

An interesting fact about decision making is that most of the decisions that we make in a hurry or when under pressure lead to regrets. Handling tough decisions is not easy. Therefore, it is advisable that you should stop, think critically and make the right choice. This is why you need the 10/10/10 mental model.

Just to remind you, the 10/10/10 framework gives you an opportunity to reflect on the consequences of your actions even before you do anything. Before deciding to do anything, you will question yourself how you will feel in 10 minutes after making a particular decision. Also, you will ask yourself how you will feel 10 months after making that decision. Lastly, you will ask yourself how you will feel in 10 years.

Why is it important to ask these questions before doing anything? The 10/10/10 mental model helps you to think critically by allowing you to think in the absence of your emotions. Instead of being influenced by the thrill of your emotions, you end up thinking twice or thrice about the consequences of your decisions.

The 10/10/10 should be applicable in most areas of your life. The decision to marry, for example. Most people allow themselves to be carried away with the waves of their emotions. One minute you are dating someone and the next thing you want is to get married. Before taking any steps further, stop and use the 10/10/10 framework. How would you feel 10 minutes after getting married? Certainly, you wouldn't notice any difference. How would you feel in 10 months after tying the knot? Maybe you will still be happy and comfortable. How about in 10 years? Will you still tolerate your partner's quirks? Will you stick to them in good and in bad times?

The 10/10/10 rule can help you in profound ways to think critically about important life's decisions. So make certain that you have it in your toolbox.

Critical Thinking Skills Gained from Using Mental Models

Analytical Skills

Critical thinking will ensure that you can carefully assess something. This could be a statement, set of information, or a problem. A critical thinker will examine things in detail by asking questions, analyzing data, seeking information, being skeptical, etc. Therefore, analytical skill is one of the main skills that you will gain by learning how to think critically.

Communication Skills

Obviously, you will spend most of your time interacting with other people either at home or at work. Consequently, it is vital that you share your ideas in a way that can be understood. Moreover, your communication skills will have an impact on how people perceive you. Critical thinking will guarantee that you can communicate effectively through asking important questions, providing reasonable explanations and arguments, enhancing your verbal and written communication skills.

Creativity

Critical thinking will also push you to embrace the idea of second-order thinking. This means that you will think at a higher level than other people. This gives you the opportunity to tap into the unknown. Therefore, you will be more creative as you will often come up with ideas, conclusions, and arguments that other people have not thought of.

Open-Mindedness

Critical thinking also demands that one should set aside their assumptions, beliefs, emotions, and attitudes. This creates a thinking space where one is open for anything. Such open-mindedness ensures that you maintain your objectivity when evaluating ideas.

Problem Solving Skills

More importantly, you will solve your problems faster. Through your analytical skills, you will have the ability to look at your problems from different perspectives. Moreover, since you will be using different forms of mental models, you will always settle for an optimal model that suits a specific situation.

In a word, critical thinking is an important skill that can help you make smart decisions. The mere fact that you can improve on how you interpret things shows that you can easily solve your problems. A critical thinker will always want to follow a logical path that leads them to the right decisions. Therefore, by using some of the mental models that have been outlined in this section, you can be sure that you will transform your life.

It is, however, important to note that it takes practice for you to hone your critical thinking skills. This means that you have to continuously apply mental models in everyday decision-making. Don't wait until you are faced with a problem for you to remember the importance of mental models. Make it a habit to stop and consider the most applicable mental model that can help you. In the end, you will make informed decisions that will guide your life in the right direction.

Chapter 6: Mental Models for Success

In life, there are those individuals whom we always seem to admire. These folks often have no problem succeeding. To them, success is just something that they can decide to do and it comes their way. However, others find it difficult and we have to try all sorts of strategies to get it right. At times, this leaves us asking: what is special about individuals who succeed easily in life? The interesting thing is that there is nothing special about these people. In fact, they are just like you and me. If you are thinking that they have more time, well, obviously, we all have the same time. The truth is that they think differently.

This chapter takes a look at how mental models can help you succeed in life. Success will come your way only if you learn how to think in the right way. But before that, let's draw a line between how successful people think and how you think. Knowing the difference can shed some light on what you ought to do to improve enhance your thinking.

How Successful People Think

They Are Specific

Successful people think differently because they are specific. These people know what they are after and how to get it. When setting goals, they will strive to be as specific as possible. In this case, they specify what their goals are without being vague. For instance, when setting a goal to lose weight, they will set a goal to lose a specific number of pounds within a particular period of time. Therefore, setting a goal to lose weight isn't enough for them.

The importance of setting specific goals is that it ignites your mind to think about the best actions that you can take to achieve your goals. Being specific about what you want also guarantees that you are motivated to fight for it. It makes your goals realistic and achievable both in the short and in the long run.

They Learn Continuously

Successful people understand the importance of learning. Earlier on, in chapter 4, we looked at compounding knowledge mental model. Warren Buffet spends most of his time feeding himself with knowledge that drives his businesses to succeed. He stands out from the crowd because he doesn't consume expiring information. Similarly, there is a lot that we have said about having many tools in your toolbox. Concerning mental models, you should ensure that you gain insights on how to apply several in your daily life.

They Grow Emotionally

Affluent people also know how to deal with their emotions. They understand the value of emotional intelligence. By learning how to recognize their emotions, they find it easy to make sound decisions. Emotions can influence how you think in many ways. Instead of thinking clearly, you might end up making hasty decisions that you could end up regretting.

Prosperous individuals strengthen their emotional intelligence by understanding that they don't have to be perfect to succeed. Moreover, they are always ready to embrace change in their lives.

They Meditate

The habit of meditation has become popular over the past few years. It is something that celebrities have popularized. The truth is that meditation has proven to have numerous benefits with regard to our thinking abilities. Meditation can help you lower your stress. In addition, it connects you to your inner self. As such, you get to know yourself better. Meditation can also enhance your brain functions.[41] Therefore, successful individuals choose to make meditation a habit because it improves the quality of their lives in profound ways.

They Work on Their Thinking

Well-to-do individuals comprehend that thinking is a discipline. For that reason, they always strive to improve on how they think. Judging from the mental models that

---

[41]"15 Reasons Why Meditation Will Make You Successful - Lifehack." https://www.lifehack.org/articles/productivity/15-reasons-why-meditation-will-make-you-successful.html. Accessed 16 Aug. 2019.

we have discussed, thinking calls for practice. Every day you have to put into practice the mental models outlined in this guide. They will guide you to make the right decisions even when faced with challenging situations.

They Focus Their Energy

In addition to the above, successful people know where to focus their energy. Warren Buffet is a good example. He uses the circle of competence mental model to focus his time and energy on areas where he is an expert. Similarly, we have talked about how the Pareto principle can help you prioritize your tasks and increase your productivity. Living a productive life doesn't mean that you should spend most of the time working. According to the Pareto principle, 20% of your efforts account for 80% of the results you get.[42] Therefore, successful people understand that you can achieve more by doing less.

They Follow Through with Their Ideas

We've heard thousands of success stories about how people decided to quit their 9 to 5 jobs to follow their

---

[42]"Pareto Principle Definition - Investopedia." 19 Jul. 2019, https://www.investopedia.com/terms/p/paretoprinciple.asp. Accessed 16 Aug. 2019.

dreams. Indeed, prosperous individuals are daring. They will go after their dreams without allowing anything to come in the way. This doesn't mean that they always thrive in what they do. However, they believe in learning from mistakes and trying again.

So, do you still think that you are different? The habits mentioned above are things that you can learn to do. If you haven't been thinking differently, then this is what might have been preventing you from succeeding.

Now, let's consider how mental models can help you change your thinking and think as successful people do.

Confirmation Bias and Success

Confirmation bias will affect the way you think in many ways. The beliefs that you have embraced will have an impact on the decisions that you will make. The decisions that you will be making will largely depend on what you believe. For instance, if you believe that it is good to live a healthy life, then you will prefer to buy healthy snacks over junk foods. Confirmation bias will also affect the people you choose to communicate with. The same case applies to your career. You will have certain perceptions that will hinder you from succeeding in life.

How Confirmation Bias Affects You

- Seeking Information

One of the main ways that confirmation bias will affect you is through the way you seek for information. You should realize that your biases will influence the perceptions that you have about the world around you. Consider a scenario when you are at home feeling bored. It is likely that you will want to waste time on social media. Scrolling through the pictures of your friends on social media will give you the impression that other people are enjoying life. Comparing such exciting lives to yours, you will gain the impression that you live a boring life. So you develop an assumption that you are a loser. There is nothing good that comes out of you. Already, you have developed some level of biases about yourself and the life you live.

Your biasness prevents you from feeling happy about yourself. Therefore, you choose to laze at home the whole day feeling bad about yourself. This shows that you opted to seek information that confirms the beliefs you have embedded in your mind. Ultimately, this affects your productivity.

- Interpreting Information

Similarly, confirmation bias will have an impact on how you choose to interpret neutral information. Your interpretation will often favor your beliefs. Take an ordinary example of someone falling in love. Well, it will be easy to assume that you are in love because you choose to see your partner as beautiful and kind. There are no flaws that you will see since you choose to only see the good side of the other individual.

Interestingly, when things fail to work, you only see the worst side of the individual you once loved. There is nothing good that you will see in them and you will end up regretting why you met them. In this situation, you should notice that it is the same person that you are dating. So what changed? It is the perception you have that changed how you view things.

- Remembering Things

Confirmation bias will also affect your memories. The beliefs embedded in your mind will influence how you recall things. For instance, when playing soccer the end result is that there is always a team that will win. If you asked people about a specific game, they will have different opinions about how the game was played. Some will argue that a particular team was better than the other. Others will say that the referees were not fair. Essentially, confirmation bias is what affects our memories.

Overcoming Confirmation Bias

It will not be easy to succeed in life if you spend most of your time seeking clarification about your beliefs. If you think that you're always wrong, confirmation bias will only drive you to seek evidence to confirm that you will never be right. This means that you will always develop a negative attitude about yourself and your life. Below are ideal solutions to help you overcome confirmation bias.

- Approach Life with Curiosity

Most people pay too much attention trying to be right in what they do. Often, they will want to work to prove themselves right among other people. Sadly, this only leads to stress and depression when they are wrong. To avoid this, it is imperative that you approach life with curiosity. Instead of trying to find perfection in everything that you do, why don't you enjoy what you do and embrace the experience that comes with it?.

The advantage gained here is that you will want to try things out without focusing too much on whether you will get it right or wrong. This means that you will not be afraid to engage in business because you fear failing. Rather, you will want to establish a business and encourage yourself that you will learn something from it. Consequently, you will fill your mind with positive energy about everything that happens to you.

- Think About Thinking

Overcoming confirmation bias also demands that you should be aware about your thoughts. Your self-awareness will help you recognize when you are formulating assumptions based on your beliefs. It is important that you learn how to recognize these thoughts and prevent yourself from believing that they are true. For instance, when browsing through the internet, it is easy to come across information that will leave you thinking, "Aha, this defines the choice I make in life!" Such assumptions will only deter you from living a happy life. Ensure that you separate yourself from the cognitive biases that you will be developing from time to time.

- Understand Varying Viewpoints

Having different viewpoints about something will improve your decision-making. It is important that you learn about the distinct mental models and how they can help you succeed in life. Varying mental models will give you an opportunity of looking at the world around you from different lenses. For that reason, you stand a better chance of making the right choices. The more you make smart decisions in your life, the easier it will be to succeed.

Clearly, confirmation bias will influence how you view the world around you. Overcoming confirmation bias might not be easy since your mind will always want the easy way out. However, when making big life's decisions, it is worthwhile that you comprehend how such biases can prevent you from making the right decisions. Your awareness will guarantee that you recognize your thoughts and separate yourself from them. They are just thoughts and assumptions and they should not define how you live your life.

Improving Productivity with Parkinson's Law

From what we had discussed earlier, the Parkinson's law argues that work expands to consume the amount of time that it had been assigned. Practically, this happens to most people. You have an assignment to complete within a week, but you postpone doing it until the last minute. Usually, many people find themselves completing their activities at the last minute. The Parkinson's explains why this happens as it points out that work will expand to fill in the allotted time. Therefore, if a certain task can be completed in a day, but you had the whole week to complete it, there is a good chance that you will complete it after a week.

With regard to productivity, people always yearn to live productive lives. However, to most individuals, they find that they have little time to manage all their daily activities. It is for this reason that you will find most people wishing that they could have more time assigned to them. The reality is that we all have 24 hours daily. Therefore, it is up to us to find practical ways of using this little time productively.

By understanding Parkinson's law, people can change how they do things and use their limited time wisely. In this case, one will realize that giving yourself more time to complete a certain task doesn't guarantee that you will finish it on time. The worst thing is that you will only waste a lot of time and still finish a project in the last minute. Consequently, the best thing that you can do to boost your productivity is to set short deadlines. This demands that you ought to limit the amount of time you spend working on a particular task. You will push yourself to beat the small deadlines while at the same time finding more time to work on other important activities.

There are several tips that should help you when using Parkinson's law to boost your productivity.

Apply the Pomodoro Technique

The Pomodoro technique was introduced by Francesco Cirillo, an author and entrepreneur in the early 1990s.[43] Essentially, the technique revolves around the idea of breaking down a large task into smaller tasks. These small tasks can then be handled in small time intervals called the "Pomodoros." The system also requires that

---

[43]"The Pomodoro Technique 101 - Lifehacker." 2 Jul. 2014, https://lifehacker.com/productivity-101-a-primer-to-the-pomodoro-technique-1598992730. Accessed 18 Aug. 2019.

one should take short breaks in between the Pomodoros. The benefit of using this system to work on large tasks is that it helps to train your brain to concentrate for a short period before continuing to work. Moreover, you will be more productive as you will find it easy to beat deadlines fast.

The short breaks advocated by the technique also guarantees that you are fueled up to continue working for longer. When setting time for each task, the system recommends that you should work for 25 minutes before taking a five minute break. After completing four working cycles (Pomodoros), you should take longer breaks of about 15 to 30 minutes.[44] Evidently, the Pomodoro technique will boost your productivity since you will strive to eliminate distractions when working.

Track Your Time Usage

If you are concerned about your lack of productivity, then it is high time that you track your time usage. Similarly, if you find that you need more time to complete tasks in your to-do list, then there is something that you are doing to take away your productive time. Your productivity will only improve after

---

[44]"The Pomodoro Technique 101 - Lifehacker."

you are aware of your time usage. This means that you should consider tracking how you spend time. After evaluating how you spend time, you will notice that you waste a lot of time on unnecessary tasks. At the end of the day, this is what affects your productivity. So, it is prudent that you work on tracking your time usage every day.

Take Breaks

Most people get caught up with the idea of being productive and they push themselves to work for longer hours. Interestingly, working overtime could be a sign that you don't know how to manage your time effectively. Accordingly, before claiming that you want to increase your productivity by working overtime, you should consider the importance of prioritizing tasks. Likewise, taking breaks gives your mind an opportunity to reboot and regain energy to continue working. Therefore, it is not a wise idea to spend the entire day behind your desk with the hopes of finishing more tasks.

Set Deadlines

To ensure that you don't waste time in a project that could be completed within a short period, you should consider setting shorter deadlines. If you have a week to complete a project, reduce this to three or four days. Working to beat the short deadlines will create more time for you to work on other important assignments. Undeniably, you will be happy that there is more that you can achieve in less time.

The Parkinson's law is simply based on the notion that you can achieve more by preventing yourself from procrastination. Giving yourself more time to work on an assignment isn't as helpful as you might think. In fact, it often leads to unproductivity since you will end up wasting a lot of time. Why should you give yourself more time when you know perfectly that you will complete a project at the last minute? As such, the earlier you complete it, the better.

Improve Decision-Making with Eisenhower Matrix

There are numerous instances where professionals have to make important decisions that affect their careers. Similarly, every individual is always making a decision before doing anything. Therefore, this is an important thing for almost everyone. When people make their choices, sometimes they think that they are dealing with pressing matters. In the real sense, some of the choices they make are not as important. Others are urgent whereas some are not. Depending on your career, there are plenty of decisions that you may need to make. As a result, you need the Eisenhower matrix mental model to help you differentiate between what's important and what's urgent.

According to Dwight D. Eisenhower, there are two problems linked to time management. These are knowing the important and the urgent. In this case, there are certain things that are important but not urgent. Similarly, not everything that we perceive as urgent is important. Understanding how to differentiate between the two can help one in effectively managing their time and improving their productivity.

There are four quadrants on the Eisenhower matrix box. Each quadrant represents a system where you can classify tasks based on whether they are urgent or important. The matrix box provides people with a helpful system of time management. When using this framework, one would tend to question themselves about the decisions that they will be making. For instance, before prioritizing anything, the Eisenhower matrix advocates that you should ask whether a task is important or whether it's urgent. Weighing the options will help you make the right choices on how you will handle the activities.

Important and Urgent

Activities that fall in the first quadrant are classified as "important and urgent." Here, the model recommends that tasks in this section should be handled immediately. This quadrant brings together urgent and important tasks. As such, activities here should be handled as soon as possible.

Important but not urgent

The second quadrant of the Eisenhower matrix features the "important but not urgent" tasks. In this section, you will find tasks which might not be urgent, but in the long run, they add value to the organization or to your personal life. For instance, you can include tasks such as working out, visiting the dentist, meditation, etc. Sure, these tasks are important, but you can schedule to do them later. The point here is that there are certain tasks which should be completed. However, it is not a must that you finish them immediately. These tasks can wait for a later period. So, consider scheduling them as recommended.

Not important but urgent

The third quadrant consists of tasks classified as "not important but urgent." Interestingly, most have plenty of these tasks in their everyday routines. You might think that these tasks are urgent, but in reality they are not relevant to your daily goals. For instance, when you are busy working using the Pomodoro technique, you might get a call from an unknown caller. Yes, it's urgent, but it's not as important as you think. The same goes to the idea of constantly checking your smartphone after every notification.

It is important to realize that there are certain decisions that are influenced by the urgency from other people. This means that they are not your priorities, but someone else's priorities. As such, attending to these tasks right away only implies that you will be allowing other individuals to come in the way of your time management. Often, people find it daunting to say no. You might gain the impression that saying no will only make you look bad. The truth is that you should learn to say no respectfully.

When handling tasks which can be classified under the third quadrant, you should either avoid them or delegate. Avoiding means that you should get rid of any distractions that could prevent you from focusing. Your smartphone, for example, it's not a must that you keep checking each and every notification that comes in. Resist the temptation by choosing to focus on your work.

Not important and not urgent

The fourth quadrant of the Eisenhower model describes tasks which are simply optional. Some of the activities that we waste our time doing are not important. They only consume our productive time. It is imperative that you monitor how you spend your time and find out whether there are tasks that fit in this quadrant. Browsing through social media pages is a good example of activities that should be classified in this category. Oftentimes, people waste their time on social media without realizing that they are wasting time.

The worst thing about spending your productive time on social media is that you never seem to realize that the clock is ticking. Instead of working on a project, you find yourself chuckling on posts from your friends. Before you know it, 30 minutes have gone and you haven't done anything. This leaves you with a lot of pressure at the end of the day. Consequently, you will want to compensate for the lost time by working overtime.

Avoid this by learning how to classify your tasks using the Eisenhower matrix box. Working overtime only shows a clear sign that you are not managing your time effectively.

Make Smart Decisions with the Circle of Competence

There is a lot to learn from Charlie Munger and Warren Buffett with regard to how people can improve their thinking. The circle of competence mental model is based on the notion that you should strive to find an area in your life where you think you are naturally strong and focus on it. This is your area of expertise. Sometimes we waste a lot of time and energy concentrating on tasks or careers that we are not good at. The effect of this is that it leaves us with a lot of pressure to keep up. We end up struggling to meet our goals in life.

The circle of competence, advocates that you should find your area of expertise and focus on it. In a way, this sounds like specialization. Concentrating your efforts on one particular area guarantees that you perfect what you are doing. You transform yourself to become the best in your own world. Ultimately, this ensures that you make smart choices that are in line with your goals.

Succeeding in life largely depends on how you make decisions. If you are a good decision-maker, you are likely to live a happy and blissful life. This is because you will always accomplish your set goals. However, this doesn't come on a silver platter. You ought to change how you think using the mental models discussed in this chapter. First, you should realize that the perceptions you hold in your mind will have an impact on how you view the world around you. Accordingly, you should utilize confirmation bias to separate yourself from your personal beliefs. Give yourself an opportunity to experience life as it comes. Don't make assumptions that will only drive you to think negatively about everything.

With regard to productivity, always have it in mind that being busy doesn't mean that you are productive. Similarly, completing many tasks in a day also doesn't account for your productivity. Productivity is determined by your effectiveness to complete tasks. Therefore, using the Eisenhower matrix model, you should learn to differentiate between important and urgent tasks. This will give you insights on how you can prioritize important tasks and delegate others. All in all, success is heavily reliant on how you use your productive time.

Chapter 7: Mental Models for Personal Life and Relationships

What do happy and successful people think about most of the time? Take your time to think about this question critically. After that, take a step back and consider whether you also think in the same manner. Well, you might make a wild guess that successful people spend their time thinking about their goals. Also, these people spend most of their productive time focusing on improving their lives. In other words, they are always optimistic about life. Are you also optimistic about your life? Do you spend your day thinking positively or negatively? How does this affect your life and the relationships you share with other people?

There is a common notion that successful people believe to be true that thoughts become things. Usually, this is a common notion meant to inform people that what they think about is what they become. Truly, it makes a lot of sense when you give this a second thought. When you spend your time thinking about all the good things that life has to offer, you will find yourself smiling and going through your day full of energy. Conversely, when you wake up in the morning feeling stressed, this will affect your day. You will want to blame everyone around you for the misfortunes that you are experiencing. The truth is that, you are what you think. For that reason, changing your thoughts can change your life and that of others.

Key Areas Affected by Your Thoughts

Before getting into detail about how mental models can help you transform your life and your relationships, let's take a moment to discuss key areas affected by your thoughts.

Your Self-Esteem

The way you think will have a profound influence on your self-esteem. Evaluate your thoughts for a moment and reflect on some of the things that you have been thinking about. Maybe you have been paying too much attention on the areas where you are not good at. It could also be that you have been stressing about the fact that things are not running smoothly in the business that you just established. Besides that, chances are that you have been trying to compare your life with that of your friends or colleagues.

Thinking too much about the negative aspects of your life only lowers your self-esteem. It diminishes the confidence that you have in yourself and your abilities. Remember the confirmation bias mental model that we discussed in Chapter 2? Focusing your thoughts on areas where you think you are incapable only confirms to your mind that what you believe about yourself is true.

Why should you put yourself through this pain? Negative thinking will only drain away your positive energy. You will never have the drive to strive for your goals. What's more, your relationships with other people will be negatively affected. This is because there is nothing good that you see in the world around you. Therefore, you will want to separate yourself from the rest of the world. Ultimately, with isolation comes depression. You will feel alone in this world, something that you created for yourself by choosing to think negatively.

Moral Standard

It is worth stressing on the fact that you are what you think. Happy people will not waste their time thinking about all the bad things about this world. Emotionally, this only affects how you perceive other people and the world around you. Your thoughts will affect your moral standards. If you are happy about life and that you enjoy every moment you live in this world, you will want to live a healthy and successful life. Have you ever wondered how successful people find time to exercise and still handle their busy schedules? Well, they believe that it is also important for them to be healthy and fit to approach the hustle and bustle of their lives. Lazy people will always complain about the lack of time. This is because they waste their time doing unimportant activities.

Your morals will tell a lot about how you think. Similarly, your thoughts will define your morals. So, changing how you think will eventually affect the moral standards that you uphold.

Inner Peace

Finding peace within and without yourself is everybody's desire. We all yearn to be happy by first finding peace within ourselves. Once you achieve this, you will find it easy to communicate with other people and express yourself naturally. However, when you lack peace, you lack joy. You will never be happy as you are always anxious about your life. Often, you will realize that you are not sure about how your life can turn out. The worst thing is that, you will feel as though you have lost control of your life. Who knows, maybe you have lost control because you don't control how you think.

Taking control of your thoughts will help you gain control of your life. Remember, you are what you think. For that reason, if you grasp a firm control of how you think, then you will have taken control of your life. It's simple, yes, but daunting to accomplish. Luckily, there are numerous mental models that you can use to make smart decisions.

Success or Failure

People who enjoy success in their lives have an interesting way of looking at things. While you might be skeptical about establishing a business, a successful individual will want to learn from their mistakes. To them, making mistakes is part of the long journey to the land of success. Consequently, they never consider mistakes from a negative perspective. Rather, looking at their mistakes positively gives them the energy they need to keep trying until they achieve their goals.

Therefore, success or failure is dependent on the direction that you choose to think. If you think that starting that business is difficult, then most certainly it will be a challenge for you. However, if you think that it is worth the try, then you will want to learn something from what you will be doing. Basically, mental models such as the confirmation bias and the map is not the territory can help you attract success to your life by simply changing how you think.

Impact on Other People

Living a life full of bliss can be gauged on the type of relationships that you share with other people. We all have limited time in this world. Therefore, the impact you live behind could tell a lot about the type of person that you are. Most billionaires that we strive to emulate have a legacy to leave behind. Individuals such as Bill Gates have helped millions of people through their philanthropic activities.

Usually, your thoughts will affect how you would want to relate with other people. If you fall in love with the world around you, you will want to help other people feel good about themselves. In the end, you will share fruitful relationships with other people.

Change Your Thinking, Change Your Life

Change Your Thinking

There is a lot that you need to consider with regard to changing your thoughts with the intention of changing your life. Right from the time you were born, there are certain self-concepts that you develop about yourself. After birth, you develop a sense of identity. What you choose to believe about yourself determines who you are. We have said it repeatedly that your thoughts define who you are.

We are all born and raised with varying beliefs. The beliefs that you have embedded in your mind will have a huge impact on what you choose to believe about yourself and your life for that matter. Bearing this in mind, it is imperative that you separate yourself from beliefs that tend to limit you from realizing your potential. You need to realize that these perceptions are rarely true. They are mere assumptions formulated in your mind.

Unlocking your full potential requires that you challenge the beliefs that tend to bring you down. This means that you should always strive to convince yourself that self-limiting beliefs are mere assumptions and they cannot determine the direction that your life will take. You have an unlimited potential. Therefore, it is up to you to unlock this potential and welcome success in your life.

The process of changing your mind will not be complete without learning how to control your self-talk. Your inner dialogue will provide you with the affirmations that you need to think clearly. Consequently, it is important that you always find a way of reminding your inner person that you love and feel good about yourself. The idea here is that you need to convince or command your subconscious mind that you are in control of your thoughts. With time, you will notice a positive change in your life and the world around you. You will realize that everything conforms to your expectations. Well, this is the power that you have within you. You create your world. So, it is best that you learn how to fill it with all the good things that you want in your life.

Change Your Life

Changing your life starts by changing how you think. Thinking positively will allow your mind and body to overflow with energy to help you approach life with happiness. There is power in positive thinking. At no time will you feel that you are not confident to handle the everyday challenges that you have to tackle. On the contrary, negative thoughts evoke negative emotions. Most of the time you will feel that you are tired living. This is because your goals seem farfetched and you cannot achieve them. Your relationships will also suffer. Certainly, you will feel suffocated and the best you can do is to give up.

So, what kind of thoughts will you choose to allow in your mind, positive or negative? The main reason why you should ask yourself this question is that you hold the power to make a choice. Your life depends on the choices that you make. This boils down to your thoughts. Choose to live a positive life full of energy by simply changing how you think. It's that simple.

Maybe you are worried about the negative thoughts that keep flooding in your mind. Frankly, we cannot deny the fact that negative thoughts are powerful since the mind often resorts to such negative thinking. Regardless, the inversion mental model can be helpful here. When you find it difficult to deal with negative emotions, you can reverse your thinking and use it to your advantage. What this means is that you can use your negative thinking to identify the hurdles that could prevent you from reaching your goals. Therefore, you will be in a better position to remove the obstacles that could deter you from unlocking your full potential.

Changing your life also demands that you should stop justifying. Why should you hold yourself captive of your emotions? Creating reasons to justify your misfortunes will only prevent these emotions from departing your mind. It is important to realize that justification will not help you in any way. If you fail in something, accept and move on. Learning to let go is an integral part of changing your life. The last thing that you should do is to deprive yourself of happiness by allowing negative feelings to settle in your mind.

Another crucial thing that is worth mentioning is the fact that people often allow themselves to be moved by the opinions of other people. There are times when we think that other people's actions were meant to hurt us. This might not be the case. The reality is that people have their own problems to deal with. Therefore, their actions should not affect you in any way. Allowing their actions to affect how you feel shows that you are not in control of your emotions or thoughts. As such, you need to challenge this by recognizing that people will always talk. You cannot prevent them from living their lives as they wish. However, you can control how you react toward what they do.

Work Hard to Achieve Your Goals

Setting goals and working hard toward achieving them are two different things. Most people set goals for the sake of it. You set goals just to convince yourself that you are working hard toward something. However, the issue arises when it comes down to doing that it required to meet the set goals. With regard to transforming your life, it is important that you work hard to achieve your set goals. Below are vital pointers that should help you accomplish your life's goals.

Decide on What You Want

The first step that you should take when looking to achieve your goals is to decide on what you want. Start by asking yourself what you really want in your life. We are all different and, thus, your goals will vary from other people's goals. Therefore, when setting your goals you shouldn't be influenced by what other people perceive as success. You are the creator of your own world. As such, the goals you set should clearly define who you are and what you aim to achieve in life.

Write Down Your Goals

When people talk about setting goals, you will often find then arguing that the best way to create goals is by writing them down. It is quite rare to find individuals arguing that memorizing your goals will help you keep motivated. Numerous studies have shown that there is power in writing down your goals. Statistics show that people who usually write their goals have higher chances of achieving them as compared to those who don't.[45] Therefore, if you have been setting goals without finding the need to write them down, you should reconsider spending time to record them somewhere.

Make a Commitment

---

[45]"The Power of Writing Down Your Goals and Dreams | HuffPost." 14 Sep. 2016, https://www.huffpost.com/entry/the-power-of-writing-down_b_12002348. Accessed 19 Aug. 2019.

There is one true fact that holds when it comes to achieving your goals; you have to be willing to pay the price. There is no shortcut to accomplishing your goals. You simply have to be committed to the process. Maybe you are struggling to dedicate your time and energy toward your goal. If this is the case, then you need to go back to the drawing board and start afresh. Chances are that you haven't set the right goals. Moreover, you should also strive to find the right motivation to keep you going.

Make a Detailed Plan

Once you have set your goals, you should come up with a realistic plan of how you are going to work toward accomplishing the set goals. It is crucial that you develop a practical plan as this will have an impact on whether you will be self-driven toward your goals. If set unrealistic goals, then you will be discouraged to keep trying when things seem impossible. As such, crafting a realistic plan will act as a roadmap to guide you from the beginning to the end.

Do Something Daily

Realizing your long term goals should be perceived as a sum of the little things that you do daily. Once you set clear goals, you should be committed to try and do something every day. You're on a mission and the best thing that you can do is to put your mind to it.

Never Give Up

More importantly, you should never give up on your dreams. You can't expect your journey to success to be easy. There will be challenges along the way. You will make many mistakes. Some will be small, but some will threaten to bring you down. Regardless of what happens, your eyes should be set on the price. Stop and think about the life that you will live after accomplishing your goals. Undeniably, there is a rewarding feeling in knowing that there is a lot in store for you if you kept going. So, nothing should stop you from realizing your dreams. The only thing that can stop you is yourself. Don't be the barrier to your happiness. Instead, channel all your energy into the process of achieving your goals.

Supercharge Your Thinking with Mental Models

To this point, you should be convinced that what you think is actually what you become. If you choose to think about your bad situation right now, chances are that you will remain in a cycle where you always struggle to solve your problems. On the contrary, if you developed the right mindset that you always solve your problems easily, then you will have the ability to solve these problems. It all depends on how you think. Mental models can help you enhance your thinking. Accordingly, this will also have a positive impact on your life and relationships.

So, how should you apply mental models to transform your life and improve your relations with those around you?

Regret Minimization Framework

Regret minimization framework is attributed to Jeff Bezos. With the help of this mental model, you can change how you think. When looking at any situation that you are currently facing, you should imagine yourself in the future after making a decision relating to your problem. Consider whether you will regret making the decision after a specified number of years. If you feel that you will regret not making a decision, then you should do that which you believe will make you happy. Of course, if you would regret not doing something in the near future, then it implies that what you choose to forego will likely make you happy.

Applying this principle to your relationships, think about how you relate with other people. In business, for example, you should reflect on whether or not you will be successful in the future if you took up the opportunity and partnered with a certain individual. You might not be as successful as you anticipated, but if the experience is worth your time, you should not hesitate to join forces. The same framework can be used to determine whether you should enter into romantic relationships with other people. Imagine yourself in the future with the person you think you are in love with. Will you regret not settling down with them? Will you regret not exchanging vows with them? If yes, then you should put your mind to it and believe that anything is possible if you believe.

10/10/10 Rule

The 10/10/10 rule is also highly applicable in your efforts to change your life and improve your relationships. This model is similar to the regret minimization framework since it allows you to think about your future. When using this model to supercharge your thinking, you should take a step back and ask yourself three important questions. The three questions reflect on how you would feel in three different time periods. First, you should question how you would feel 10 minutes after deciding to do something. Secondly, consider how you would feel 10 months after making your move. And third, reflect on how you would feel in 10 years.

When entering into any serious relationship, use the 10/10/10 to evaluate the decision that you are about to make. How will you feel in 10 minutes after making that important decision? What about in 10 months or in 10 years? It is crucial that you turn to mental models to help you think clearly without being blinded by your emotions.

Second-Order Thinking

Second-order thinking also reiterates the importance of thinking about the consequences of your actions or decisions even before doing them. However, second-order thinking mental model stresses on the fact that people should not regret making mistakes. You cannot predict the future. Therefore, you shouldn't evoke negative emotions that will only drain energy from you. The best thing that you can do is to learn from your mistakes and move on. The beauty of life is that you can try to do something for as many times as you like. The right mindset will ensure that you benefit from the experience that you gain from the mistakes you make.

Your critical thinking skills will be put to use when using the second-order mental model. Before doing anything, take a step back and reflect on the effects of your decisions. After that, you can follow your instincts if you feel that there is something good to gain from what you will choose to do.

To put it briefly, your life depends on how you think. When you finally realize that you are the creator of your own world, you will tap into the power of changing your life. A mere change of thoughts can miraculously transform your life. You will live a life that you have never experienced before. Living a blissful life should be based on the material things that you have. Instead, it starts by changing how you think. This shouldn't be a daunting task since there are plenty of mental models that you can turn to. These models will supercharge your thinking and help you make informed decisions about your life.

Chapter 8: Strengths and Weaknesses of Mental Models

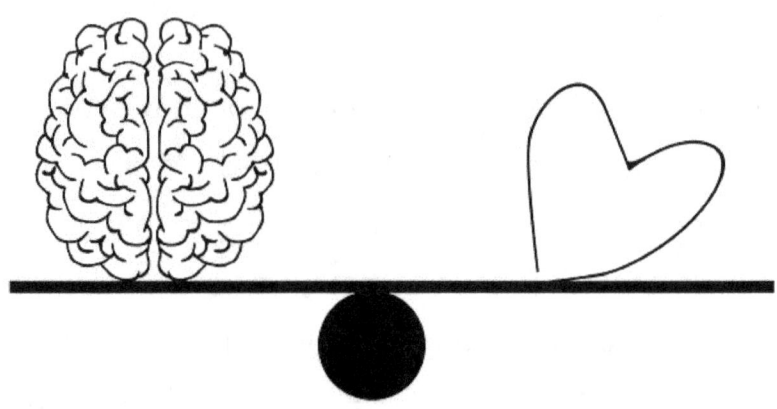

One of the main benefits of mental models that can be clearly outlined from this guide is that they help you change how you think. Mental models will provide you with multiple ways of viewing the world around you. As such, you garner a deeper understanding of how to interpret things. The way you think affects your life in many ways. Therefore, by mastering how to think critically, you can influence your life in an ideal way. However, it is worth noting that there are certain weaknesses of mental models. Some of these frameworks are applicable in certain instances where others are not. Moreover, some models are easy to comprehend whereas others are complex. This section discusses more about the strengths and weaknesses of mental models. In addition, there are pointers that will be outlined to help you circumvent common challenges experienced when using mental models. Read on!

Strengths of Mental Models

The overall advantage gained when using mental models is that it allows one to think better. Generally, the quality of your thinking will rely on the number of mental models that you have in mind. Just to remind you, mental models are distinct ways of understanding the world. People will have varying views of the world. It is from their perceptions that they formulate their ideas of how things should be. In other words, mental models are there to simply the complexities of this world.

There are numerous types of mental models. The ones that have been discussed in this manual are the best that you can find. However, it is important to note that people can develop their own mental models. Depending on what you choose to believe, you can come up with a framework that helps you to simplify what you perceive as complex in your own little world. Accordingly, the bigger picture of using mental models is that it ensures that people can think better and make sound decisions.

The strengths of mental models can further be broken down into smaller categories. Some of these strengths are as discussed below.

Understand the World

Mental models will transform your perceptions about the world around you. When using these models, you will realize that the world around you makes more sense. Why? This is because you will have a unique way of explaining what is going on around you. Consider a scenario where people didn't understand the world around them. Undeniably, it creates a situation where it is difficult to make crucial decisions about our lives.

The mental models that people have created in their minds help them to conform and live communally. When people have shared beliefs about a particular aspect, they will effectively relate to each other. It is easy to make friends with like-minded people because you share similar ideologies.

With regard to the notion of helping people understand their worlds better, mental models will vary depending on their effectiveness. There are several factors that will affect how mental models are used.

- Knowledge

The level of people's understanding about a certain model will have an impact on whether they will choose to use it or not. If they are conversant about the mental model in question, then they will want to apply it in real life. However, individuals who find themselves struggling trying to figure out what the models mean will be discouraged from applying these models. For that reason, users should equip themselves with the right knowledge about mental models. Reading and comprehending these models is just not enough. You should put into practice what the mental models recommend.

- Attitudes

The attitude that you have toward mental models and their effectiveness will influence your decision on whether you will be relying on them. The shared beliefs that people have about a particular concept will determine the choices they will be making. Some will be rigid to change their mindsets. On the other hand, some would be willing to embrace change in their lives.

- Environment

Our external environment is always transforming how we think and what we choose to believe. These are the people around us, technology and geographic dispersions. Your parents raised you in a way that makes you stick specific ways of doing things. In the absence of mental models, you would be too rigid to change. This is because your mind doesn't allow you to believe in something that does not conform with the perceptions embedded deep within.

Information technology has brought about numerous changes to the world we live in today. People are consuming information at a high rate as compared to years before. Unfortunately, some of the things that we choose to consume only corrupt our minds. Consuming the wrong information not only affects your morals, but it also changes how you think. For instance, spending too much time on things that spur negativity will only influence you to think negatively. If you spend most of the time watching violent films, there is a good chance that you will become violent. The environment around us will thus have an impact on how mental models are utilized.

Taking into consideration the factors discussed, there is a certainty that some mental models will work better than others in distinct situations. People who are exposed to an environment where they have to deal with distractions from technological devices will find it difficult to use mental models to their advantage. Conversely, those who have learned how to discipline themselves in the midst of all external distractions will use mental models effectively. That's not all, people who acknowledge the importance of mental models will develop a sense of curiosity on what other models propose. Hence, they will focus on learning more mental models to boost their critical thinking skills.

Weaknesses of Mental Models

Mental models are indeed helpful more so with regard to improving how we think. Nonetheless, it begs to question why most people don't use them. Equally, you might wonder why these models might not be effective when applied by other people. You might find yourself in a situation where you are applying mental models, but things fail to work as expected. Some of the weaknesses of mental models can help you in understanding what prevents them from being significant.

Absence of Guidance on Model Use

Mental models might fail to work when applied by other people because of the limited guidance that they can find. Sure, it is easy to claim that mental models will help to improve how you think. However, some folks will desire for something more to gain a deeper insight into mental models and why they are important. Fortunately, this guide has not only discussed what mental models are, but it has also provided you with practical examples of how you can apply these models in real life.

Patience and Constant Practice

After learning about the different types of mental models that you ought to have in your toolbox, you shouldn't stop there. These models will not work if you only read them and forget about them. It is vital that you learn how to connect with your thoughts and identify instances when you can best apply the mental models. For instance, when going through a challenging situation, this is a good time to reflect on some of the models in your toolbox and evaluate their applicability. This way, you will be using the tools in your toolbox for the right purpose.

Mental Models Supercharge Each Other

Additionally, mental models could fail to work when one has limited knowledge about the types of mental models. Certainly, a carpenter will not successfully complete their job if they went to work with just a hammer. In the same manner, you will not realize a positive change when using mental models if you only learn one or two. To change your life and solve your problems faster, you should invest in learning more about the different forms of mental models. This means reading books such as this and living a mindful life by knowing when and where to use them.

Strengths and weaknesses of mental models should help you realize that there are times when the models you use might fail you. When this happens, you should not give up on them. Keep in mind that successful individuals such as Warren Buffet, Jef Bezos and Charlie Munger are using them. Therefore, you should change your strategy and use the right tools for their intended purpose.

Chapter 9: The Relationship Between Mental Models

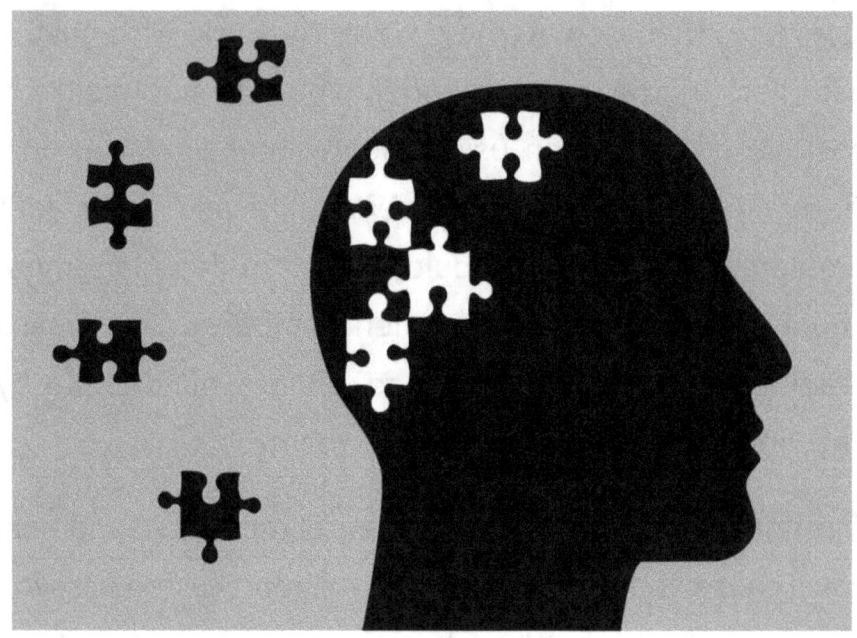

As a newbie in using mental models, you might find yourself trying to figure out the best criteria that you can use to choose the best mental models. Certainly, there are numerous models out there. What we have discussed in this guide are the best models that you should consider using. Nevertheless, it is important to tip you on the right strategies that you should use when picking models from different disciplines.

Tips to Choose the Right Mental Model

You will be surprised to learn that there are hundreds of mental models out there. However, this doesn't mean that you should learn all of them. The best mental models will be the ones that you find applicable in your life. This means that your selection process should be based on the applicability of the mental models. If they are not applicable, try to limit yourself to the few that will have an impact in your life.

There are plenty of mental models from different disciplines ranging from Economics, Psychology, Chemistry to Engineering. In the world of economics, for example, you will come across comparative advantage as one of the mental models. Other thinking frameworks that you will find here include economies of scale, supply and demand, diversification, common knowledge, game theory among others. In Psychology, you will find reciprocity, tribalism, status quo bias, loss aversion, anchoring and illusion of control. The point here is that there are numerous mental models from varying disciplines.

So, how do you determine that you are choosing the best model among the many that you will be learning about?

Relevance

One of the most important things that you should consider when choosing the right mental model is its relevance. After reading and understanding what a certain model means, you should ask yourself whether it applies to your life. If the model doesn't help you in any way, you should consider focusing your attention on what's most important. Accordingly, strive to compare between different mental models by considering their relevance

Clarity

When comparing between different models, you will want to settle for a framework that can help you think clearly. For you to achieve this, you have to understand what the framework is all about. If the message is not clear, this might make things worse since you could end up misinterpreting what he model advocates for. Misinterpreting the mental models will affect your critical thinking skills as well as the decisions you will make. The worst thing is that you may end up arguing that mental models are not effective. Consequently, it is vital that you mull over the clarity of the models you intend to choose.

Variety and Conformity

The more mental models you have in your toolbox, the more effective you will be in solving problems and making sound decisions. This demands that you should spend time learning about different models from varying disciplines. When doing this, an important thing to recall is that the models you choose should work harmoniously. For instance, the model you select from the Economics field, should not be in contrary to what another model from Psychology advocates for. The idea here is to prevent yourself from getting confused. If one mental model says this and the other says something else, this could only make it difficult for you to make informed decisions.

To be on the safe side, choose mental models that complement each other. The last thing you need is to waste your time trying to figure out which mental model is preferable.

Know What the Truth Is

It is also critical that you know what the truth is about a particular matter. Knowing the truth will help you discern between realistic models and those that are not. As you go about using different types of mental models, you ought to realize that some models have not been scientifically proven or they have not been widely accepted. So don't believe anything that comes your way unless you prove with reliable evidence.

Understand the Pros and Cons of Each Model

Before picking any model that you find applicable to your life you should take a look at the pros and cons of the model. Getting a deeper insight about these models will help you identify some of the potential pitfalls of using a certain framework. For instance, there are specific models which are based on unrealistic assumptions. Some assumptions are scientific assumptions that you cannot make. Therefore, it would be unreasonable to have such models in your toolbox.

Picking the right mental model will determine whether or not you find it useful in your life. For that reason, you should think twice about the frameworks that you will be selected to add them to your toolbox. Like any other prudent carpenter, they will always strive to pick the right tools that serve them better. Therefore, ensure that you don't fill your toolbox with tools that you will not be using.

Chapter 10: Mental Models Toolbox

Besides using models to help you change and improve your thinking, you should also consider using varying forms of thinking tools from distinct professions. When you think about what engineers do, the first thing that would come to mind is that they build things. For economists, you will associate them with money. When looking at these professions from a different perspective, there is something else that you can learn from them. In this case, instead of paying attention to what they do or the problems they deal with, try to figure out how they solve their problems. By doing this, you will unveil an array of thinking tools that you might not have thought about before. This chapter dives in to look at different professions and the thinking tools that you can borrow from them.

Artist: What if Creativity Took Precedence

Many professions out there have their limitations. In most cases, you will find that experts are often driven by monetary gains. However, in art, this is somewhat different. Before your piece of art can sell, the first thing that you ought to polish is your creativity. This means that creativity comes before the profits that you expect to gain from your artwork. Now, using this thinking tool, consider how your career would change if at all you prioritized creativity instead of monetary gains. Would your career be any different? What about your goals, would you alter your goals to ensure that creativity takes precedence?

Entrepreneur: Rapid Prototyping

Another critical thinking tool that you can borrow from entrepreneurs is their notion of doing many things at a go with the hopes that some will work. This system of doing things can be termed as rapid prototyping. This strategy is based on the idea that you come up with a product and introduce it into the market to determine if people want it. Using this idea, you can apply it to various aspects of your life.

When trying rapid prototyping in real life, your aim is to try different things and see what works. Before making up your mind to do something, you should try out different options without raising high expectations as to whether it will work. While doing this, it is imperative that you pay attention to feedback. Consider what people are saying about what you are doing. If you are launching a business, positive comments will be a clear indication that you need to go big. The importance of this critical thinking tool is that it gives you an opportunity to make several mistakes and settle for the best alternative that serves you best.

Doctors; Using Symptoms

Doctors have a unique way of finding out what their patients are suffering from. The first thing that a doctor would do is to evaluate you based on how you are feeling. A patient, therefore, has to inform the doctor about the symptoms that they are experiencing before any medications can be prescribed. Judging from what a patient is saying, a doctor is required to gather information and figure out the most likely ailment that one is suffering from. Accuracy is of great importance here. If a doctor makes a wrong diagnosis, it could lead to serious health consequences or even death. Therefore, crucial decisions have to be made.

A thinking tool that you can borrow from this profession is the notion of using symptoms to diagnose diseases. Applying this to real life events, you should always solve your problems by first checking the symptoms that you are experiencing. If your manager is complaining about your productivity, find out the main reasons why you think your manager is complaining. Maybe you always arrive late to work or that you have not met the expected deadlines. Using these symptoms, you can then deduce what is affecting your productivity. Here, you can argue that you need to work on time management.

Journalist: Fact-Checking

Journalists try their best to ensure that what they are reporting is nothing but the truth. To do this, they have to rely solely on facts. This means that if there is anything that appears vague, they would opt to leave it out as it could be classified as fake news. Preventing such misleading information is the main goal of a journalist. The aspect of fact-checking is an important thinking tool that you can borrow from them.

With regard to decision-making, how would you gather information that you need to make informed choices? Using the fact-checking thinking tool, you should focus on choosing the right tools that will help you in making smart decisions. So, don't go around picking junk and expect to make sound decisions. Stick to facts.

Accountant: Ratio Analysis

Ratio analysis is a critical thinking tool that you can take from the accounting profession. Ratios compare between two varying measurements. Ratio analysis refers to the quantitative techniques used to gain insight into liquidity, profitability and operational efficiency of a company.[46] Using this thinking tool, you can create ratios that can tell you more about your debt to income difference. Also, if you are setting goals to lose weight, you can come up with ratios to tell you more about the amount of calories you should consume against what you should lose daily.

Evidently, there is a lot that you can learn from different professions. You should remember that your goal is not to think about the types of problems that they have to deal with. Rather, your attention should be on how they solve their problems. Taking this perspective will help you learn many things from a wide array of professions.

---

[46]"Ratio Analysis Definition - Investopedia." 13 Jun. 2019, https://www.investopedia.com/terms/r/ratioanalysis.asp. Accessed 19 Aug. 2019.

Final Thoughts

Congratulations on reaching this point of this book. There is a lot that you have grasped about mental models and their significance. We live in a world full of complexity. There are numerous things that we interact with daily, but sometimes we fail to understand their importance in our lives. Moreover, people are always faced with the challenge of making decisions. Often, we are told that happiness is a choice. When going through challenges in life, it is daunting to think of the fact that life is purely based on the decisions that we make. The guide has provided you with a comprehensive look into how your life can be greatly influenced by how you think.

A common phrase that you might have come across is the fact that you are what you think. What this means is that people are defined by their thoughts. What you think about most of the time is what you eventually become. Practically, this makes a lot of sense. When you tend to focus your attention on thinking negatively, you attract negative things in your life. You will always be blinded by the negative experiences that you might be going through.

On the contrary, when you choose to think positively about any situation that you might be going through, you will find the energy you need to free yourself from the situation. People always make mistakes. There is nothing that you can do without making slight or big mistakes here and there. Unfortunately, some people focus too much on these mistakes and they end up thinking that they cannot succeed in life. The reality of the matter is that you are the creator of your own little world. Therefore, if you choose to tune your mind to focus on the good side of life, you will enjoy your life to the fullest.

Mental models are there to help us deal with the complexities of this world. Different people have varying ways of understanding the world around them. The frameworks that they use to understand certain things is what is termed as mental models. These models provide us with an easier way out of our problems. If there is a problem that you might be facing, using mental models can guarantee that you solve your problems with ease.

Prior to reading this manual, you might have asked yourself about the significance of mental models. When making decisions, it is not uncommon to get lost not knowing the right direction to take. Usually, this occurs due to our limited knowledge of certain events that we are faced with. The worst thing that could happen is that people make poor decisions that affect their lives. For instance, when starting a business, having the right capital could motivate you to jump into a certain business idea without thinking of the challenges and opportunities that you could take advantage of in the market. Depending on the mental model that you use, it will provide you with a reason to take a step back and think twice about your decision.

In conjunction to what has been said, mental models are there to make sure that you have confidence in the approach you will use to make your decisions. The models that you will be using have been used by successful individuals out there. Some of them have been proven scientifically. Accordingly, there is a high probability that you will make informed choices when using mental models.

That's not all, having the right framework to use also gives you a clear direction that you should follow to end up with the right decision. Knowing that there is a certain strategy to follow in your decision making process is crucial. You stand a better chance of making systematic decisions. There is a wide array of mental models in different disciplines. Some of these models are quite relevant to your day to day life. You shouldn't fret that there are many models that you haven't mastered for you to improve your thinking. The important thing is for you to gain a firm grasp of how to use the best models that have been discussed in this guide.

The Pareto Principle is a common mental model that you will find it easy to understand and apply. This principle can have a profound impact on your productivity if you used it right. According to this model, 80% of the results you get are attributed to 20% of your efforts. This means that working the whole day is not the best way of living a productive life. Similarly, it doesn't mean that you should be lazy when attending to your daily routines. The point here is that people should realize that productivity is not gauged by the number of tasks that are completed. However, it is determined by how effective you are in completing these tasks. Completing many tasks in a day would only mean that you are efficient. The issue here is that you could end up completing tasks which are not important. So, ensure that you prioritize your to-do list and make sure that you handle the most important tasks first. Other assignments can be delegated or scheduled as recommended by the Eisenhower matrix model.

Another vital model that is highly applicable with regard to managing your time wisely and boosting your productivity is the Eisenhower matrix box. This framework will help you draw a thick line between important and urgent tasks. When using this model, you will realize that there are certain tasks which are important but not urgent. As such, it is best that you schedule to work on these tasks at a later time. Similarly, some tasks are not important, but urgent. The best way of handling these tasks is by delegating them. They are not important, however, it is necessary that you complete them on time. Knowing how to manage your time wisely using the Eisenhower mental model will ultimately help you to live a productive life. You will have more time to spend with your family and friends. The best part is that you will never find yourself complaining that you need more time to complete tasks in your to-do list.

Another effective model that you should always remember to apply in everything that you do is the 10/10/10 rule. This model is applicable in many areas of your life. Whether in business, education, relationships, etc. You can rely on this framework to help you in making the right decisions. The mere fact that this model is also simple to use makes it admirable. You only need to ask yourself three questions based on how you will feel after deciding to do something. You will consider asking yourself how you will feel 10 minutes, 10 months and in 10 years if you decided on something. Think about it this way, giving a second thought about your decisions ensures that you separate yourself from emotions which could cloud your judgement. Accordingly, you end up making smart choices. This mental model works like the second-order thinking model.

The exciting aspect of mental models is that you will never run out of tools to incorporate in your toolbox (mind). For instance, say you have a problem trying to overcome negative thoughts. In such a situation, the best model to use would be the inversion mental model. This framework gives you the opportunity of turning your negative thinking to your advantage. If you are thinking about the factors that could prevent you from reaching a specific goal, you should realize that the mind is giving you hints on things that you should avoid. So, to ensure that you don't fail to accomplish your goals, you only need to avoid the factors that you have been thinking about. Take note of the fact that it takes practice for you to master how to use these mental models. Therefore, don't expect to change your mind right from the word go.

What's more, you should also bear in mind that your limited knowledge could prevent you from realizing the positive impacts of using mental models. Thus, it is highly recommended that you take your time to learn most of them and practice using them when making important decisions in your life. A powerful strategy that you should also remember to use is to use varying models together. This is because there are several models that supercharge each other. Therefore, understanding one model can help you in clearly comprehending what the other means.

To put it concisely, change your thinking and change your life. It's that simple, but it requires patience and constant practice from your end. Good luck!

References

Argument: Claims, Reasons, Evidence. (n.d.). Retrieved from https://www.comm.pitt.edu/argument-claims-reasons-evidence

Bloem, C. (2018, February 20). Why Successful People Wear the Same Thing Every Day. Retrieved from https://www.inc.com/craig-bloem/this-1-unusual-habit-helped-make-mark-zuckerberg-steve-jobs-dr-dre-successful.html

Bradford, A. (2017, July 25). Deductive Reasoning vs. Inductive Reasoning. Retrieved from https://www.livescience.com/21569-deduction-vs-induction.html

Charles T. Munger Quotes (Author of Poor Charlie's Almanack). (n.d.). Retrieved from https://www.goodreads.com/author/quotes/236437.Charles_T_Munger

Compounding Knowledge. (2019, February 12). Retrieved from https://fs.blog/2019/02/compounding-knowledge/

The Danger of Oversimplification: Use Occam's Razor Without Getting Cut. (2019, July 28). Retrieved from https://fs.blog/2017/05/mental-model-occams-razor/

Finding Your Own Circle of Competence: The Difference Between What You Think You Know and What You Actually Know. – Drift. (2019, June 12). Retrieved from https://www.drift.com/blog/circle-of-competence/

First Principles -BJJ Mental Models. (2019, April 29). Retrieved from https://bjjmentalmodels.com/first-principles/

Frost, A. (n.d.). Mental Models: The Ultimate Guide. Retrieved from https://blog.hubspot.com/marketing/mental-models

Hanlon's Razor: Relax, Not Everything is Out to Get You. (2018, August 31). Retrieved from https://fs.blog/2017/04/mental-model-hanlons-razor/

Henry, A. (2019, July 12). Productivity 101: An Introduction to The Pomodoro Technique. Retrieved from https://lifehacker.com/productivity-101-a-primer-to-the-pomodoro-technique-1598992730

Hoffman, J. (2018, April 5). How I Live My Life With Mental Models. Retrieved from https://medium.com/@jaymehoffman/7-mental-models-i-live-my-life-by-e79742d4f074

How Maslow's Famous Hierarchy of Needs Explains Human Motivation. (2017, April 20). Retrieved from https://www.verywellmind.com/what-is-maslows-hierarchy-of-needs-4136760

How Ratio Analysis Works. (2006, May 1). Retrieved from https://www.investopedia.com/terms/r/ratioanalysis.asp

How to be More Productive by Using the 'Eisenhower Box? (2019, August 12). Retrieved from https://jamesclear.com/eisenhower-box

Intro to Myers-Briggs Personality Types. (2017, February 18). Retrieved from https://www.referralsaasquatch.com/myers-briggs-personality-types/

Kaufman, J. (n.d.). Parkinson's Law. Retrieved from https://personalmba.com/parkinsons-law/

Khandelwal, N. (2018, January 6). Maslow's Hierarchy of Needs vs. The Max Neef Model of Human Scale development. Retrieved from https://medium.com/@hwabtnoname/maslow-s-hierarchy-of-needs-vs-the-max-neef-model-of-human-scale-development-9ebebeabb215

Kim, S. (2017, June 8). 3 Decision-Making Models Used by Warren Buffett and Jeff Bezos. Retrieved from https://www.inc.com/sean-kim/how-warren-buffett-and-jeff-bezos-make-smarter-decisions.html

Latticework of Mental Models: Thinking From First Principles. (2018, March 16). Retrieved from https://www.safalniveshak.com/latticework-of-mental-models-thinking-from-first-principles/

The Map is Not the Territory: How to Improve Your Judgment – Patrik Edblad. (2019, July 19). Retrieved from http://patrikedblad.com/mental-models/the-map-is-not-the-territory/

Marble, D. (2018, March 27). Jeff Bezos Quit His Job at 30 to Launch Amazon--Here Are the 3 Simple Strategies He Used to Do It. Retrieved from https://www.inc.com/darren-marble/jeff-bezos-quit-his-job-at-30-to-launch-amazon-heres-how-to-know-if-its-right-time-for-your-big-move.html

Maslow's Hierarchy of Needs - Physiological, safety, social. (2014, May 23). Retrieved from http://thepeakperformancecenter.com/educational-learning/learning/principles-of-learning/maslows-hierarchy-needs/

Mental Models: The Best Way to Make Intelligent Decisions (109 Models Explained). (2011, August 2). Retrieved from https://fs.blog/mental-models/

Metacognition. (2018, May 7). Retrieved from https://cft.vanderbilt.edu/guides-sub-pages/metacognition/

Mueller, A. (2014, July 7). 15 Reasons Why Meditation Will Make You Successful. Retrieved from https://www.lifehack.org/articles/productivity/15-reasons-why-meditation-will-make-you-successful.html

The Pareto Principle Explained. (2003, November 24). Retrieved from https://www.investopedia.com/terms/p/paretoprinciple.asp

The Power of Writing Down Your Goals and Dreams. (2016, September 14). Retrieved from https://www.huffpost.com/entry/the-power-of-writing-down_b_12002348

The Principles of Comparative Advantage. (2018, June 9). Retrieved from https://fs.blog/2009/08/should-tiger-woods-mow-his-own-lawn-the-principles-of-comparative-advantage/

Rana, Z. (2018, February 23). The 10/10/10 Method: Make Decisions Like Warren Buffett and Ray Dalio. Retrieved from https://medium.com/personal-growth/the-10-10-10-method-make-decisions-like-warren-buffett-and-ray-dalio-99e4857d05e3

The Role and Power of Mental Models. (2014, April 30). Retrieved from http://integralleadershipreview.com/11428-role-power-mental-models/

Surfing or 'Riding the Wave? (2018, September 25). Retrieved from http://bestmentalmodels.com/2018/09/25/surfing-or-riding-the-wave/

Understanding Opportunity Cost. (2003, November 24). Retrieved from https://www.investopedia.com/terms/o/opportunitycost.asp

Why Employers Value Critical Thinking. (2014, November 26). Retrieved from https://www.thebalancecareers.com/critical-thinking-definition-with-examples-2063745

Your logical fallacy is ad hominem. (n.d.). Retrieved from https://yourlogicalfallacyis.com/ad-hominem

www.ingramcontent.com/pod-product-compliance
Lightning Source LLC
Chambersburg PA
CBHW070635220526
45466CB00001B/178